The Crystal Fix

In loving memory of my father, James Thornbury,
a true gem whose kind and creative spirit
continues to inspire today.

Brimming with creative inspiration, how-to projects and useful information to enrich your everyday life, Quarto Knows is a favourite destination for those pursuing their interests and passions. Visit our site and dig deeper with our books into your area of interest: Quarto Creates, Quarto Cooks, Quarto Homes, Quarto Lives, Quarto Drives, Quarto Explores, Quarto Gifts, or Quarto Kids.

First published in 2019 by White Lion Publishing, an imprint of The Quarto Group.
The Old Brewery, 6 Blundell Street
London, N7 9BH,
United Kingdom
T (0)20 7700 6700
www.QuartoKnows.com

This edition first published in 2021
Text and Photography © 2019 Juliette Thornbury
Design by Ginny Zeal
Cover design by Louise Evans

ISBN 978 0 7112 6868 5
Ebook ISBN 978 1 78131 813 3

10 9 8 7 6 5 4 3 2 1

Printed in China

DISCLAIMER:
The information in this book is for informational purposes only and is not intended as a guide to replace the advice of a counsellor, physician or medical practitioner. There is the possibility of allergic or other adverse reactions from the use of any crystals mentioned in this book. You should seek the advice of your doctor or other qualified health provider with any questions you may have. You should not use the information
in this book as a substitute for medication or other treatment prescribed by your medical practitioner.
    The authors, editors and publisher make no representations or warranties with respect to the accuracy, completeness, fitness for a particular purpose or currency of the contents of this book and exclude all liability to the extent permitted by law for any errors or omissions and for any loss, damage or expense (whether direct or indirect) suffered by anyone relying on any information contained in this book.

The CRYSTAL FIX

HEALING CRYSTALS FOR THE MODERN HOME

Juliette Thornbury

WHITE LION
PUBLISHING

CONTENTS

INTRODUCTION

My passion for crystals began early in life. My mum would take me and my sister to local markets when we were young and I always eagerly sought out the crystal stall; I still remember the purple velvet tablecloths beneath hundreds of glimmering stones. This is where my crystal collection began, and I still have my first little agate geode almost twenty years later. My grandparents were jewellers, so I grew up around gemstones; appreciating the vibrant and sparkling beauty of garnet, amethyst, peridot and rose quartz, among so many others.

In 2015, I decided to turn my passion for crystals into a business. I created Luminosity Crystals, an online store selling high-quality and ethically sourced crystals and minerals from all around the world. I wanted to be able to source the stones myself and share them with those seeking an alternative healing approach or just a beautiful cluster for their home. Since that time, my fascination with crystals has developed into a full-time career and I now connect people all over the world with these powerful healing tools. The world of crystals and minerals has become an important part of my life, physically, mentally, emotionally and spiritually.

Harnessing the energy of the Earth, crystals bring balance, harmony and a sense of peace. For me, they are a catalyst to living a healthier and happier life. They encourage mindfulness and help me feel more grounded and connected to nature. Whether you use them during meditation, in full moon rituals, beauty routines or just by keeping one on your coffee table, crystals will provide you with a direct connection to yourself and your surroundings.

The Healing Power of Crystals

The healing power of crystals has been a feature of cultures and civilizations for thousands of years. The ancient Sumerians were among the first to use them in this way. They believed crystals contained magical properties and used them in jewellery and healing formulas. Ancient Egyptians adorned themselves in turquoise, lapis lazuli, quartz and carnelian, and crushed malachite and galena into fine powders for using in cosmetics. Crystals such as rose quartz and jade have been valued for their healing properties in traditional Chinese medicine for at least 5,000 years, while shamans and healers from the ancient indigenous cultures of South America, North America, India and Australia have also long included crystals in ceremonies and rituals as a way of connecting with the spirits and with the Earth.

So, how do crystals work? Each has an energy field that can positively interact with your own, naturally directing, absorbing, amplifying and focusing energy within the body. Like all things in the universe, crystals run on vibrations; each one embodies a unique energy with a range of positive attributes depending on the type, colour and vibration of the stone. Working with crystalline energy assists in restoring the body to its natural state and helps to bring into balance all aspects of the self. This results in a healthier mind and body, a more positive outlook and a higher quality of life.

Studies have demonstrated that some crystals also conduct energy. In 1880, French physicist Pierre Curie discovered 'piezoelectricity'. He found that putting mechanical pressure on various stones, including quartz and topaz, generated electricity. This is why crystals are used extensively in electronic appliances today, including computers, mobile phones and TV screens, as well as skin care products and medical equipment.

I believe that intention and level of consciousness encourage a person to be receptive to the healing power of stones. When we are more aware of the different vibrations around us, we are able to feel the effects they have on our lives. From alleviating stress and anxiety with amethyst to promoting abundance and success with citrine, crystals are powerful tools that we can use in many ways to create positive shifts in our lives.

Crystal Formation

Crystals form naturally in the Earth's crust when magma travelling upwards from the core starts to cool down. This process of crystal formation can take billions of years and is known as crystallization. Differences in temperature, pressure and chemical composition are all factors that influence the type of crystal that forms. Impurities can also affect a crystal's chemical make-up and colour. For example, quartz crystals are naturally clear, yet the presence of iron or manganese compounds add a vibrant purple or pink colour, creating variations known as amethyst and rose quartz.

Minerals, Rocks, Crystals and Gemstones

The terms mineral, rock, crystal and gemstone are often used interchangeably, however each one indicates significant structural differences.

MINERAL

A mineral is a naturally occurring solid substance that contains distinct crystalline structure and chemical compositions. While not all minerals are visible crystals, they do contain crystals in microscopic form. There are more than four thousand identified minerals, each with its own characteristics and structure. A mineral is identified by five specific characteristics: it must be naturally occurring, inorganic (though there are some exceptions, such as coal), it must be a solid at room temperature, have a definite chemical composition and an ordered internal structure. Each of these characteristics must be present for a substance to be identified as a mineral.

ROCK

Rock is composed of several minerals combined, and does not contain the specific chemical composition that would normally be found in a mineral. Rocks can also include other organic remains, as well as mineraloids – substances similar to minerals that do not demonstrate crystallinity.

CRYSTAL

Most minerals occur naturally as crystals. A crystal is a solid material made up of ions, atoms and molecules arranged in an orderly repeating pattern. Crystal structure can influence the physical properties of a mineral, including its colour, lustre, texture and form.

GEMSTONE

A gemstone is a valuable mineral or crystal that has been cut and polished, often to use in jewellery and other adornments. The value of a gemstone depends on quality, size, rarity and colour.

How to Use This Book

The Crystal Fix is a modern guide to crystals and minerals, offering a unique insight to the powerful healing properties of a wide range of stones and how to harness their energies. Use this book as a guide to discover the mental, physical and spiritual benefits of incorporating crystals into your daily life.

Finding a Crystal to Match Your Need

There are a number of ways in which you can use this book to find the right crystal for your needs. At the heart of the book, the stone directory 'The Crystals' (see pages 48–151) discusses over 60 individual stones in detail and is organized in sections according to key healing properties, whether they are for Love & Relationships or Health & Wellness, and so on. You can also turn to the 'Stones By Need' index (see pages 184–88), which identifies common concerns, from depression and anxiety to fear of flying and insomnia.

Crystals in the Home

The first chapter is a complete introduction to crystals and includes a guide to using crystals to create positive energy flow within your home. This section is organized according to the key rooms in the home, to help you find specific stones that match up with the energy you want to attract into a particular space. This chapter also discusses the various shapes and sizes of crystals, along with information on crystal care and the different ways to cleanse and charge your stones.

Using Crystals

Chapter three provides step-by-step guides to key rituals, crystal grids and essences to enhance crystal healing. This section introduces crystal-infused beauty routines to promote healthy, glowing skin, as well as massage treatments and other healing methods that can be enhanced by incorporating crystals. Chapter three also discusses the benefits of using crystals to bring balance to the energy centres of the body – known as chakras – and provides a detailed description of the stones that correspond with each chakra, along with their colour associations and healing attributes (see pages 164–65).

CHAPTER 1

LIVING WITH CRYSTALS

Selecting Crystals for You

With there being thousands of different crystal varieties to choose from, selecting the perfect one can seem overwhelming. If you feel drawn to a specific crystal, it can often mean that you are in need of that stone's particular energy in your life. Here are a few helpful methods to assist you in selecting the right ones:

BY COLOUR: If you are looking to acquire a stone for a particular need, it can be helpful to choose the stone by its colour, for each carries an energy that is related to its colour. For instance, pink and green stones are associated with the heart chakra and are powerful in aiding emotional healing. You may like to look up the colours and their associations first (see page 165) or pick the one that you are drawn to. Either way, selecting a crystal by its colour is an effective way to ensure you are choosing the right stone for your needs.

BY FEEL: Many people like to choose crystals based on how they feel. By holding a stone and focusing on how its energy feels, you will be able to decide whether you are connected to its healing vibration. Some people feel a hot or cold sensation emanating from the stone. Others may feel its energy resonating with a certain chakra or a specific area on the body. This method may take some time to develop, so remember not to feel pressured if you have not yet become fully attuned to this ability.

BY NEED: Crystals can be great sources of comfort and support in all kinds of circumstances. If you are going through a difficult time emotionally, a stone such as rose quartz can bring great comfort and peace. If you are looking for a stone to increase energy, creativity or motivation, carnelian may be the stone for you. You can use the index at the back of this book to search for stones that answer particular concerns or requirements (see pages 184–88).

Crystal Shapes and Sizes

Crystals come in a huge range of shapes and sizes – factors that have a unique effect on a stone's healing energy and how it can be used for the best results. Some of these shapes occur naturally, while others have been artificially cut and polished to create a new formation. Learning the purpose of each shape, as well as the difference between polished and raw stones, will greatly enhance your knowledge of how and when to use each variety.

Polished vs Raw Stones

Being unaltered, raw crystals tend to carry a stronger energy than those that have been cut and polished. Polished stones carry a softer vibration that can be helpful for many situations, especially for those who are sensitive to crystal energies. Both raw and polished stones are effective healers and have an important place in any crystal collection. Be aware of the different energies that each type can stimulate when selecting your crystals to make sure they align with the purpose you wish them to fulfil.

Crystal Shapes

There are hundreds of crystal shapes and formations, many of which are extremely popular for both healing and decorative purposes. When a stone is carved into a certain shape, such as a sphere or point, it will influence how the energy flows throughout the crystal. The following are some of the most common varieties, each carrying their own specific characteristics:

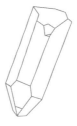

- **NATURAL POINT** A natural point is a powerful raw crystal that has not been polished or altered. These crystals are often used in healing and are powerful stones for directing energy towards or away from the body, depending on the direction in which you direct the point of the crystal.

- **GENERATOR** A generator crystal features six facets that converge at a point. This shape is known as an energy amplifier and will increase a stone's overall healing properties.

- **SPHERE** Spheres emit energy from all angles, creating an equal energy flow throughout an entire space. A sphere is a particularly effective crystal to keep in the home if you are looking to energize and purify your surroundings.

- **PYRAMID** A pyramid features four equal sides with a base. It may be natural in some cases, however many are polished into this shape. Pyramid crystals are known to deepen meditation and are effective to use when setting positive intentions or affirmations.

- **CLUSTER** Powerful energy amplifiers, clusters contain many points that come from the same base. These stones radiate energy outwards, while cleansing and purifying the space around them.

- **GEODE** A crystal geode is a hollow cave-like stone with numerous smaller terminations inside. As with a cluster, a geode will amplify the energy but will also soften it, allowing a slower release of a given energy.

- **WAND** Crystal wands are often cut and polished into shape. They are typically rounded at both ends and are popular stones among massage therapists and reflexologists. Other wands may be pointed at one or both ends, making them powerful stones for directing the flow of energy.

- **TUMBLED** These stones are usually small and polished, and are perfect to use in crystal grids, meditation, essences and other basic healing practices. Their size and durability also makes them useful stones to carry with you.

Crystal Care

Caring for your crystals is relatively simple, however learning a few tips will help you to avoid any accidents, such as disolving your celestite in water while trying to clean it. Some elements of crystal care include cleansing and charging your crystals to enhance their healing properties, as well as diferent methods for cleaning and storing your stones. It is also important to make sure you purchase your stones from a sustainable and ethical source.

Buying and Sourcing Crystals

The crystal healing industry is growing rapidly in popularity. With so many sources all around the world, both online and in-store, it can be difficult to know where your crystals originally come from and if they have been sourced ethically. The process of collecting crystals is much gentler on the Earth than the mining of industrial minerals such as graphite, corundum or limestone, as the majority are sourced by hand or by small-scale mining. Large-scale mining for precious stones is usually focused on extracting gold or copper rather than crystals, which are often considered a by-product of the more environmentally destructive industrial mining. However, it is important to be aware of unethical mining and poor working conditions, especially in relation to large-scale mines.

Crystals can also go through many hands before ending up in yours, so it is important to support the sellers that are open about where they source their stones, and to look out for those that don't disclose this information, even when asked. Of course, it can be difficult to know for sure. However, it is helpful to look for a supplier that understands and respects where the stones have come from. By building strong, lasting relationships with crystal suppliers you can establish a high level of trust regarding authenticity. By remaining conscious and mindful when sourcing crystals, we can ensure that the natural environment is appreciated and preserved.

Cleansing and Charging

Crystals accumulate negative or stagnant energies and is it important to cleanse and charge them regularly, especially stones that are used for healing of any kind. Doing so restores a crystal's natural frequency. There are various methods for cleansing and charging your stones.

- **SMUDGING** Burn palo santo wood or a sage smudge stick and hold your crystal in the smoke to cleanse its energy. This a powerful ancient practice that has been used for centuries to clear negative energy and connect us to the spirit world. Today, both sage and palo santo are seen as essential tools for energy cleansing and other sacred rituals.
- **MOONLIGHT / SUNLIGHT** Lay your crystals out in the sun from dawn until dusk, or leave them overnight under a full moon to recharge. Remember that some crystals, such as amethyst, may fade in harsh sunlight. Moonlight, however, suits all types of crystals.
- **WATER** Place your crystals under fresh running water for several minutes to cleanse and energize them. This method is not suitable for delicate or porous stones, such as celestite.
- **OTHER CRYSTALS** Some crystals can be used to cleanse and recharge other stones. Selenite is my favourite example of this, as it carries a powerful cleansing and purifying energy. Placing smaller crystals on top of a selenite crystal overnight will cleanse and recharge their energy. This is also an ideal cleansing method for your crystal jewellery.

Cleaning Your Stones

While many crystals can be cleaned in running water, some, such as selenite, are water-soluble. Fragile or porous stones may be cleaned with a dry cloth or using an aerosol air duster. It is best not to use harsh chemicals to clean your crystals, as this can damage their surfaces and even affect their energies.

Displaying and Storing Your Stones

When displaying or storing your crystals, be mindful of those that may fade in sunlight. These include fluorite, amethyst, citrine, smoky quartz, rose quartz, green apophyllite, celestite, aquamarine, topaz and kunzite. Delicate crystals that may easily scratch or chip can also be stored in a cloth or a bag to protect them when not in use. This is also helpful for fragile crystal jewellery that may otherwise be damaged when kept amongst other stones or jewellery.

TRY THIS

Use amethyst in an essence (see page 172); take a few drops under the tongue to help with nerves and to alleviate jet lag. Alternatively, you can place an amethyst crystal in a water bottle to sip on throughout the day.

Travelling with Crystals

From protecting against accidents to calming nervous flyers, carrying crystals with you when travelling is a powerful way to benefit from their healing properties. When we travel we often experience fatigue or stress, and crystals are useful tools for offsetting this. Keeping a protection stone such as black tourmaline or smoky quartz in your pocket will bring a sense of security and calmness. Hematite will keep you grounded and balanced, which is especially helpful for those who feel stressed when travelling.

Tumbled stones are ideal crystals to travel with, as they are small and can be carried conveniently in hand luggage or in a pocket. Wearing crystal jewellery is another effective way to harness healing energy while travelling. By keeping a crystal close to your body, you are able to connect with its energy, allowing the stone to positively influence your own vibration as well as the energy around you.

Key Stones for Travel

- Turquoise
- Malachite
- Moonstone
- Pyrite

- Carnelian
- Black Tourmaline
- Amethyst
- Smoky Quartz

- Garnet
- Hematite

Fear of Flying

Many people tend to feel anxious or fearful when flying, and certain crystals can be worn or carried with you to help ease these stressful situations. Malachite is a powerful protection stone that will calm feelings of anxiety or fear, while also providing relief from motion sickness and vertigo. Hold a grounding stone, such as black tourmaline or hematite, to soothe and stabilize nervous energy.

Protection Against Accidents

Pyrite and turquoise are powerful protection stones that can be used to guard against accidents while travelling. Carnelian and garnet are also known to protect against accidents and injuries, especially while driving.

TOP ROW (L-R) aquamarine, opal, ruby **MIDDLE ROW (L-R)** sapphire, amethyst
BOTTOM ROW (L-R) peridot, topaz

Wearing Crystals

Crystals have been worn in jewellery for thousands of years, for both their beauty and healing properties. Wearing a crystal is a powerful way to benefit from the stone's energy, especially when using it for a particular purpose. Having a crystal in your energy field for a long period of time will increase its ability to support your intentions and can help you to manifest whatever you need in your life.

Use your intuition when picking a stone to wear. Often, you will find that the one you select carries the energy that you need most at that time. If you are looking to attract love into your life, for example, wear a rose quartz necklace to invite this energy in. Wearing a ring or necklace with citrine will help you to attract abundance and success into your life.

To increase the energy of the stone, try wearing it over the related chakra to boost its healing effects. For example, if you are looking to strengthen communication skills, wear an aquamarine necklace over the throat chakra.

BIRTHSTONES

Twelve gemstones have come to be recognized as representing specific birth dates and are a popular way of choosing a crystal for jewellery. The stones are affiliated with a specific month of the year, and also with one of the zodiac symbols. You may therefore find that two different stones both relate to your birthday; choose the one that resonates with you the most.

BIRTH MONTH	STONE	COLOUR	ZODIAC	ASSOCIATED QUALITIES
January	Garnet	Red	Capricorn (Dec 22 – Jan 19)	Loyalty & Purity
February	Amethyst	Purple	Aquarius (Jan 20 – Feb 18)	Sincerity & Peace
March	Aquamarine	Blue-green	Pisces (Feb 19 – March 20)	Courage & Faith
April	Diamond	Colourless	Aries (March 21 – April 19)	Balance & Clarity
May	Emerald	Green	Taurus (April 20 – May 20)	Happiness & Loyalty
June	Moonstone	White	Gemini (May 21 – June 20)	Balance & Joy
July	Ruby	Red	Cancer (June 21 – July 22)	Nobility & Beauty
August	Peridot	Green	Leo (July 23 – Aug 22)	Love & Protection
September	Sapphire	Blue	Virgo (Aug 23 – Sept 22)	Wisdom & Truth
October	Opal	White	Libra (Sept 23 – Oct 22)	Confidence & Stability
November	Topaz	Yellow	Scorpio (Oct 23 – Nov 21)	Friendship & Strength
December	Turquoise	Blue	Sagittarius (Nov 22 – Dec 21)	Prosperity & Success

Crystals in the Home

Keeping crystals in the home is a wonderful way to attract positive energy into your space. They will amplify the atmosphere you need while clearing away any negativity. Placing the right stones around your house will keep spaces feeling light, positive and pure. This section of the book identifies key spaces in the house, matching each one with the ideal optimal energy and the stones that will help you to create it. Use this as a starting point then follow your own intuition to select the best stone for particular areas in the home.

Take time to consider what it is that you would like each stone to bring to the home – are you hoping to attract abundance into your home? Do you want to foster a calm atmosphere for the family space? Once you have identified your intention, use the advice on the following pages to select the stone, placement and display method that will best achieve that. To maximise the healing potential of crystals in the home, clear the space of any negative energy before introducing a new stone to your space; it can also be helpful to programme each stone with a specific intention.

Space Clearing

Stagnant and negative energy can build up in homes, whether from disagreements, bad moods or even illness. It is important to clear your space regularly, as this will promote balance and harmony within the area and will help to clear away any unwanted energy. Burning sage, incense or palo santo wood is a very effective way to cleanse the area of any negativity. Space clearing will bring the home back to its original state of peace, comfort and positivity. (See page 162 for a space-clearing ritual.)

Programming

It is important to programme your crystals, especially when you using them for a particular healing purpose. Having cleansed a stone, sit quietly and hold it in your hands for a few moments. Set your intention for the crystal by focusing on its desired purpose – for example, health, love, abundance or protection. By dedicating the crystal to a specific purpose, you are infusing it with pure intention.

Setting an intention is a powerful way to begin the process of manifesting your goals or visions. An intention can be seen as an internal drive that brings a sense of clarity and direction in life. When setting your intention for the day or week, ensure that it is positive and uplifting, for

CRYSTALS FOR A NEW HOME

Before moving into a new home, trying gridding the space with black tourmaline (see page 127). After cleansing with sage or palo santo wood, place a black tourmaline crystal in each corner of the house to create a protective shield against negative energy. Placing a clear quartz crystal in each room will amplify the positivity in your new home.

example: 'I intend to bring love and happiness into my life'. Setting an intention is about defining how you wish to operate both mentally and spiritually – not only to achieve your goals but also in bringing a greater sense of self-awareness and gratitude to your daily life.

Introducing Crystals to a Room

There are many beautiful ways to introduce crystals into the home. As with plants, crystals offer an opportunity to bring a piece of nature into your space. By exploring different placement options that are both aesthetically pleasing and practical, you will be able to immediately lighten the energy and ambience of the home. Below are some of my favourite ways to display crystals that can be applied to any area of the home, and on the following pages are room-specific ideas that will help to attract the right kind of energy into each area.

- A small dish or bowl carved from a crystal such as rose quartz is a lovely way to display jewellery or other small items, while also adding some extra positive and loving energy into your space. In the bathroom, it can be used as a soapdish.
- Keep quartz points or clusters on a surface where the sun regularly shines; this will often create a stream of beautiful rainbows, transforming your living area into a bright and positive atmosphere.
- Use crystal bookends on shelves to brighten up your favourite reading corner, or to keep stagnant energy away from the office space.
- Crystals also work well with houseplants to bring a fresh and earthy feel to the home or workspace. In the soil at the base of a plant or beside a plant pot are perfect places for your crystals to hang out, while also helping your plants to stay strong, healthy and happy. Green stones like aventurine, malachite and moss agate are effective for keeping in your garden or near indoor plants, along with clear quartz to amplify healing energies.

Feng Shui

Feng shui is an ancient Chinese art, dating back to over three thousand years. It is a principle based on the concept of life-force energy, also known as *chi*. This energy flows throughout our home and surroundings, while affecting our emotional, physical and spiritual bodies. By following feng shui principles, balance and harmony is achieved within a space and a positive flow of *yin* (female) and *yang* (male) energy is attained.

Following the principles of feng shui is an effective way to incorporate the use of crystals in the home. Keeping a specific stone in each area of the home will bring an ambience of harmony and balance to the space, creating an overall sense of emotional, physical and spiritual wellbeing.

The feng shui bagua is an energy map that can be used to chart the space in your home. You can use this chart to determine the energy flow in your home, office, or a particular room in the house. First, draw a basic floorplan of the space you wish to chart, then overlay the bagua map, aligning the lower end of the grid with the wall that contains the main entrance.

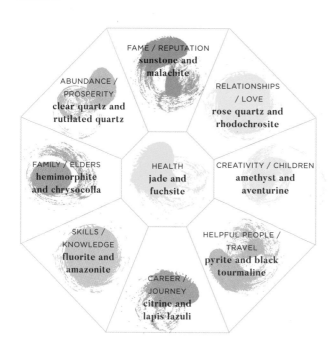

TRY THIS
To keep a hallway feeling open and inviting, place a sage smudge stick in a dish near the entrance to keep the area cleansed and free of stagnant energy.

Entrances and Hallways

The entrance to the home should carry a safe, warm and welcoming energy. As the physical marker of your personal space, you want the entryway to reflect the personality and atmosphere of the whole home. Welcome visitors to your space with warm and friendly vibes! It is also important to cleanse this space regularly as it is so often a place of comings and goings and can accumulate other people's energy.

Key Stones for an Entrance
- Black tourmaline
- Obsidian
- Citrine
- Hematite
- Selenite

Black tourmaline, hematite and obsidian are powerful stones for keeping this area of the home free from negativity; place them above the front door as a symbol of protection and comfort. Citrine is another beautiful stone for attracting warmth and happiness into the home; kept in the hallway, it will attract positivity and abundance. Placing selenite on the windowsills and in doorways will also help to create a protective barrier against negative energy while attracting light and positivity into the atmosphere.

TRY THIS
To keep your kitchen feeling fresh, use a purifying clear-quartz-infused room spray with your favourite scent (see page 173) to keep the space clean and positive.

The Kitchen

Often called the 'heart of the home', the kitchen is a social area where friends and family come together to share food, talk and interact. In modern homes, kitchens have become multipurpose spaces in which kids might do homework or families watch TV, as well as being rooms for cooking, eating and drinking. For this social hub, you want to create a nurturing energy of love, health and friendship. Stones that promote open communication and loving relationships can be particularly powerful in this area of the home.

Key Stones for a Kitchen

- Hemimorphite
- Rutilated quartz
- Clear quartz
- Rose quartz
- Apophyllite
- Aventurine
- Jade

Green aventurine and apophyllite are effective stones for encouraging an uplifting vibration of happiness, peace and wellness. Placing these crystals in a jug of water for drinking throughout the day is a powerful way to feel the healing benefits of these stones. Keeping rose quartz or hemimorphite on a windowsill, and jade among fresh herbs, will promote a healthy, nurturing environment in the kitchen, while rutilated quartz – a powerful cleansing crystal – can help to keep the energy light and clear.

THE CRYSTAL FIX

TRY THIS

Combine crystals with houseplants to promote harmony and balance within the living room, while amplifying the energies of growth and renewal.

The Living Room

Traditionally, the living room is a space of warmth and relaxation. It is important for this space to be cleared regularly – as a social area of the home, it will carry a constant flow of different energies. Crystals in the living room can be used to promote conversation and congeniality, and as such are often connected to the heart and throat chakras. They can also be beautiful objects to have on display on a coffee table or shelf – in particular, raw clusters amplify energy equally throughout the room and look beautiful.

Key Stones for a Living Room

- Hemimorphite
- Lodolite quartz
- Apophyllite
- Aventurine
- Rose quartz
- Clear quartz
- Amethyst

Apophyllite and clear quartz are powerful cleansing crystals and will keep a space free of negativity. A clear quartz cluster kept near the centre of the room will radiate positive energy while also bringing a greater sense of vibrancy to the space. As it is often centrally placed in the room, a coffee table is the ideal display surface for this stone and the cluster will make a lovely focal point.

Hemimorphite, lodolite quartz and aventurine are excellent stones for building healthy relationships, while amethyst and rose quartz will encourage a peaceful and harmonious atmosphere. Place these stones on a shelf or side table to support open communication, harmony and happiness in the home. Creating a crystal grid (see page 174) is another great way to amplify the healing energies of these stones.

TRY THIS

Use lepidolite, amethyst and clear quartz in a crystal grid (see page 174) and place it under your bed to encourage deep sleep and relaxation.

The Bedroom

The bedroom should be your own private sanctuary for rest and relaxation. Crystals can be very helpful to encourage a deep sleep, particularly those with a calming vibration. A couple of well-placed crystals in this room will be more effective than having too many, as this may cause conflicting energies. When used in this way, crystals are highly effective in promoting peace and tranquillity, while creating a warm and relaxing atmosphere. Keep the bedroom free of distracting electronics to promote a more restful sleep and to allow your mind and body to relax before sleeping.

Key Stones for a Bedroom

- Rose quartz
- Angelite
- Danburite
- Kyanite
- Amethyst

- Celestite
- Scolecite
- Moonstone
- Howlite
- Lepidolite

- Jade
- Fluorite
- Clear quartz

Calming stones such as amethyst, celestite, angelite, howlite and scolecite are perfect examples of crystals that can be kept in the bedroom to promote a balanced and calm environment. Place a howlite sphere next to your bed to bring a light and peaceful energy to the entire space. If you feel restless or stressed before bedtime, holding this stone will help to relax your mind. A rose quartz jewellery dish makes a lovely addition to a nightstand, while also promoting love and peace; a candleholder made from amethyst is a beautiful way to bring a calming crystal energy that will promote a sense of peace and relaxation.

To help with insomnia, place any of the following stones under your pillow: scolecite, lepidolite, angelite, danburite, fluorite, amethyst, howlite or moonstone. Tumbled stones are the most comfortable for this. You can also use jade, kyanite and amethyst in a similar way to encourage lucid dreaming.

A Child's Room

A child's room should carry a warm and safe energy that encourages peace and contentment. Crystals introduced to this space help provide a nurturing and comforting atmosphere for children of all ages. It is, however, important to note that small crystals may not be suitable for very young children. Toxic varieties should also be avoided, such as malachite, amazonite, vanadinite, lapis lazuli, tiger's eye and pyrite. Never leave these within a child's reach.

Key Stones for a Bedroom

- Amethyst
- Kunzite
- Black tourmaline
- Moonstone
- Onyx
- Obsidian
- Rose quartz
- Fuchsite
- Amethyst

Many children are drawn to crystals for their brilliant colours and shapes. It is important to allow them to choose their own crystals from a young age so that they can discover the different energies of each one. It is also good to find ways of incorporating crystals into fun activities, such as making personal bracelets or creating artworks. For babies, teething necklaces made from amber offer an effective way of incorporating crystals into early childhood.

Moonstone, kunzite and fuchsite are beautiful stones for young children and babies, and carry a sweet and nurturing vibration that will promote deep sleep and relaxation. Keeping an amethyst geode in the corner of the room will also release positive and calming energy throughout the space – perfect for hyperactive toddlers. For older children or teenagers, placing a black tourmaline or obsidian in each corner of the room will bring a grounding and stabilizing effect while creating a protective shield against negative energy.

Amethyst and onyx are particularly useful to guard against nightmares; place on a bedside table or in a small pouch under the bed or pillow. Alternatively, you could create a crystal grid (see page 174) to keep in the room.

TRY THIS

Place an amethyst or rose quartz crystal in a little pouch under your child's pillow or under the bed to encourage feelings of peace, love and comfort while they sleep.

The Bathroom

The bathroom should be an area in the home for rejuvenation, cleansing and recharging. Crystals can work beautifully in the bathroom, along with your favourite candles or a room diffuser to create a beautiful cleansing and purifying energy.

Key Stones for a Bathroom

- Chrysoprase
- Blue lace agate
- Shungite
- Aquamarine
- Rose quartz
- Clear quartz
- Jade
- Amethyst

A cleansing crystal such as a clear quartz cluster will bring a refreshing energy to the space. Chrysoprase and blue lace agate are beautiful water-energizing stones that carry a soothing and cleansing energy, perfect to keep near the sink or shower. Bringing a couple of amethyst crystals with you into the bath, along with a few drops of lavender oil, is an effective way to relieve stress before going to bed. Shungite is also one of the most powerful stones to purify water and to detoxify the body; place in a run bath to benefit from its powerful rejuvenating qualities.

TRY THIS

Crystals can be incorporated into your daily beauty or self-care rituals. Aquamarine and rose quartz are known for their anti-ageing properties and can be used in a cleansing face mist for a youthful and vibrant complexion (see page 173). A jade or rose quartz facial massage roller is an effective anti-ageing tool that promotes healthy, glowing skin (see page 168).

The Office

The office or workspace should carry an energy of inspiration and motivation. Crystals can be incorporated into this space to boost energy levels and creativity, while also helping to create a stress-free environment. Many people today need to adjust to multiple roles in the workplace and there are a variety of stones that can help you to adapt to these different situations.

Key Stones for an Office

- Turquoise
- Amazonite
- Citrine
- Fluorite
- Carnelian
- Jasper

- Vanadinite
- Black tourmaline
- Aventurine
- Malachite
- Tiger's eye
- Pyrite

- Smoky quartz
- Sodalite
- Hematite
- Shungite

Citrine is known as a crystal of abundance, wealth and success, making it a powerful stone to keep in the office. Placing a fluorite point in a dish near your computer will enhance productivity, focus and organization and can be a wonderful aid for students. Tumbled stones are great to keep in the workspace or by your computer to hold whenever you need to pause and re-focus your energy. Placing a smoky quartz cluster on your desk will help absorb negative energy from your environment while promoting stability, focus and mental clarity.

If you are looking for a communication stone, carry or wear a crystal that is associated with the throat chakra, such as amazonite, sodalite or turquoise. If you are nervous about an important meeting, carnelian, jasper, pyrite and tiger's eye can bring an extra boost of self-confidence and courage – keeping one of these stones on your desk can also increase energy, creativity and motivation.

Combat Electronic Pollution

When working around computers, laptops, mobile phones and other electronics, certain crystals can be very efficient in protecting against electromagnetic pollution. By wearing or placing a shielding crystal such as hematite, pyrite or shungite near your device, it can subtly neutralise the effects that electromegnetic fields have on the body. Malachite is another stone that absorbs all kinds of environmental pollutants and can be placed in front of your computer to absorb harmful energies. The following stones can all be used to protect against electromagnetic pollution and are most effective when worn on the body or placed directly beside your computer or laptop: fluorite, pyrite, aventurine, black tourmaline, malachite, vanadinite, sodalite, hematite and shungite.

Note: Be mindful of highly magnetic crystals such as magnetite and hematite; these can cause some devices to malfunction if placed too close.

CHAPTER 2

THE CRYSTALS

TRY THIS Use rutilated quartz in a crystal grid (see page 174) to bring abundance and joy into your life.

WORKS WELL WITH Rutilated quartz works beautifully with citrine (see page 55) to attract happiness and success.

Rutilated Quartz For Abundance

A powerful crystal when it comes to amplifying thoughts and intentions, rutilated quartz is one of the most effective stones for manifesting abundance and prosperity. It also has cleansing and purifying qualities, helping to remove negative or stagnant energy from its environment.

HEALING PROPERTIES

- Abundance
- Transformation
- Empowerment
- Manifestation
- Prosperity

USE FOR

With its uplifting, spiritual vibration, rutilated quartz is a helpful tool to use during meditation. It teaches patience and will help you to remain grounded and open to your own spirituality.

COLOUR AND FORMATION

Quartz crystals that contain thin threads of mineral inclusions are known as rutilated quartz. Rutile strands are usually less than a millimeter thick, travelling from one end of the crystal to the other in perfect straight lines.

HOME AND SPACE

Rutilated quartz is a beautiful stone to keep in the social rooms of the home, such as the kitchen or living room. Not only will it bring a high and positive vibration to these rooms, but it will ensure that the space is cleared and cleansed of other people's energy as they come and go.

SOURCE AND HISTORY

Rutilated quartz can be sourced all over the world, although it is most often found in Brazil, South Africa and Madagascar. Historically, rutilated quartz was most frequently used for its ability to promote psychic power and strengthen intuition.

CHAKRA AND BODY

This crystal activates the solar plexus chakra. It increases self-esteem, allowing you to feel more confident and open. Placing rutilated quartz above the belly button will work with the solar plexus chakra to help attract new energy, stability and vitality.

Sunstone For Optimism

Sunstone is a bright and energizing crystal. It is known as an abundance stone that will help to restore optimism and happiness in your everyday life. Symbolizing the warmth and strength of the sun, this stone brings self-empowerment, creativity and vitality.

HEALING PROPERTIES
- Abundance
- Optimism
- Happiness
- Creativity
- Vitality

COLOUR AND FORMATION
Sunstone forms as transparent or opaque crystals with iridescent flashes. Its warm colour can vary from red-brown to yellow-gold.

SOURCE AND HISTORY
This crystal is found in Canada, the United States, Norway, Greece, India and Russia. In ancient Greece it was thought to represent the sun god, Helios, and was believed to bring luck and good fortune to those who carried it.

USE FOR
Wearing sunstone in a necklace will help to relieve stress and to attract abundance into your life. A natural antidepressant, sunstone protects a wearer from negative energies.

HOME AND SPACE
Keep this powerful stone in the office or workspace, where it will enhance productivity and encourage the flow of new and fresh ideas. It will help you to stay focused and energized throughout the day.

CHAKRA AND BODY
Sunstone is most associated with the root and sacral chakras. This nurturing and grounding stone will make you feel empowered and full of life. Placing sunstone over the pelvic bone or at the base of the spine will foster new energy, inspiration and motivation.

TRY THIS Keep sunstone near your workstation to enhance mental clarity and motivation.

WORKS WELL WITH Together, sunstone and carnelian (see page 116) make a powerful combination for enhancing energy, sexuality and creativity.

TRY THIS Use pyrite in a crystal grid (see page 174) to attract abundance and success into your life. Place a citrine point in the abundance/prosperity corner of your home (see page 32) to attract abundance and wealth.

Pyrite For Vitality

Symbolizing the warmth of the sun, pyrite carries powerful vibrations of strength, vitality and happiness. It is a strong manifestation stone and will bring abundance and prosperity into all areas of life. It is also a powerful stone of protection, guarding against negative energy while promoting physical and emotional wellbeing.

HEALING PROPERTIES

- Abundance
- Manifestation
- Prosperity
- Success
- Vitality

COLOUR AND FORMATION

Pyrite often grows in perfect cubic or octahedral formations and emits a beautiful metallic golden hue.

SOURCE AND HISTORY

This crystal can be found in Canada, the United States, Peru, Spain, Great Britain and Italy. In ancient times, it was held as a stone of great magic and was used by Native American healers during healing ceremonies and rituals. A popular crystal to use for decorative purposes, pyrite was often carved into amulets, jewellery and other ornamental objects in ancient Greece.

USE FOR

Wearing pyrite is an effective way to increase your energy levels and to reduce mental exhaustion. It will bring inspiration and motivation to the wearer, while also attracting abundance and success.

HOME AND SPACE

This is a wonderful stone to keep in the office or workspace, as it increases mental clarity and focus while lifting the vibration of the entire room. Pyrite inspires passion and creativity in the workplace and will attract good fortune to your business.

CHAKRA AND BODY

Pyrite activates the solar plexus chakra, enhancing inner power, joy and confidence.

Citrine For Happiness

Harnessing a bright and warm energy, citrine is a stone of happiness and success. It is best known for its ability to attract joy, creativity and prosperity. Used as a cleansing crystal, citrine also clears away negative energy from its environment.

HEALING PROPERTIES

- Warmth
- Happiness
- Success
- Creativity
- Abundance

COLOUR AND FORMATION

A type of quartz, citrine grows as transparent crystals found in clusters or single points. In its natural state, it contains an earthy colour that ranges from soft yellow to deep browns. Heat-treated varieties of citrine are created artificially by heating amethyst, giving the stone a brighter orange colour.

SOURCE AND HISTORY

Treasured across many parts of the world, natural citrine is found primarily in Brazil, South Africa and Madagascar. In ancient Egypt, citrine was not only worn as a symbol of opulence and wealth but was also used to decorate weaponry. In seventeenth-century Scotland, the handles of swords were embellished with citrine, as it was believed to bring success and victory to all those who carried it.

USE FOR

Citrine is powerful when worn in jewellery, as it emanates positivity and protects the wearer from negative energy.

HOME AND SPACE

Keep citrine in the workspace to enhance energy flow and productivity.

CHAKRA AND BODY

Citrine is a stone for the solar plexus chakra. When placed above the belly button, it enhances your ability to manifest abundance and bring happiness into your life.

LEFT pyrite
RIGHT citrine

TRY THIS Jade is known as a 'dream stone' and can be a wonderful dream enhancer. Placing a small piece under your pillow may also encourage lucid dreaming.

WORKS WELL WITH Jade and turquoise (see page 138) make a powerful combination for attracting positivity and luck, and for promoting general wellbeing.

Jade For Good Luck

Jade has long been recognized as a stone of abundance, happiness and good fortune. Its energy stimulates the flow of new ideas, helping to attract success and prosperity. Jade is also known as a stone of eternal youth, bringing vitality, health and joy to one's life.

HEALING PROPERTIES

- Abundance
- Happiness
- Luck
- Healing
- Love

COLOUR AND FORMATION

Jade is formed as an opaque, or sometimes translucent, stone that can be found in multiple colours depending on its mineral composition. Although it is mostly known for its green varieties, other colours include blue, yellow, white, red, brown and black.

SOURCE AND HISTORY

Jade is found in many countries, including Canada, the United States, Russia, China and New Zealand. The stone has a rich history of use across many cultures for its wide range of healing properties. Jade is particularly valued in China, where it has long been used for carvings, statues, jewellery, ritual artefacts and even muscial instruments.

USE FOR

Known for its anti-ageing properties, Jade is a wonderful stone to add to your beauty ritual. Use a jade roller (see page 168) over your skin to increase blood circulation and promote a healthy, glowing complexion.

HOME AND SPACE

Keep jade in the office or workspace to attract abundance, wealth and good luck.

CHAKRA AND BODY

Jade is primarily connected to the heart chakra. Meditating with this stone, or wearing it in a necklace, will soothe the heart and allow you to feel relaxed, open and balanced.

Apatite For Motivation

A stone of manifestation, apatite will enhance your creativity and motivate you to work consistently in order to achieve your goals. It also aids in communication and self-expression, while boosting your self-confidence. Apatite is also an effective cleansing and purifying stone, eliminating any stagnant or negative energy from its environment.

HEALING PROPERTIES

- Manifestation
- Creativity
- Motivation
- Communication
- Intuition

COLOUR AND FORMATION

This crystal tends to form as small translucent or opaque hexagonal crystals. They are usually blue or yellow, but green, white, purple and brown variations also occur.

SOURCE AND HISTORY

Apatite is most often found in Canada, the United States, Mexico, Brazil and Russia. It was named in 1786 by German geologist A.G Werner after the Greek word for 'deceit' (*apáti*), as it was often confused with other stones such as tourmaline and beryl.

USE FOR

This is a helpful crystal to use when starting new projects or for those employed in a creative line of work. It allows you to focus and provides new insights to help you reach your full potential. If you are feeling distracted or lethargic, hold a piece of apatite to overcome energy blocks.

HOME AND SPACE

Keep apatite in the workspace to increase productivity and motivation. As a stone of abundance, it will also attract prosperity and good fortune.

CHAKRA AND BODY

Apatite is most associated with the third eye and throat chakras. It will enhance your intuition and bring clarity to the mind and emotions, allowing you to feel more open and communicative.

TRY THIS Wear apatite in a necklace
to enhance intelligence and increase your
ability to absorb new information.

WORKS WELL WITH Combine
apatite with rhodonite (see page 78) to
help improve your natural skills and talents.

Amazonite For Empowerment

With its captivating blue-green hue and powerful healing abilities, amazonite has been a popular stone for hundreds of years. Named after the Amazon River for its soothing water-like appearance, this stone carries a strong and beautiful energy that encourages empowerment and success. It is also a manifestation stone that can be used to attract abundance and good fortune.

HEALING PROPERTIES

- Success
- Prosperity
- Truth
- Courage
- Empowerment

COLOUR AND FORMATION

Usually opaque, amazonite grows in either tabular crystals or as great masses that may contain a white or grey webbing. Crystals have a brilliant blue-green colour, often with a pearlescent sheen that varies from yellow-green to bright turquoise.

SOURCE AND HISTORY

Amazonite is most commonly found in Canada, the United States, Brazil, Namibia, Madagascar and India. Seen widely as a decorative stone, amazonite was often used in the making of statues and jewellery. In ancient Egypt, it was carved into small amulets to increase fertility and attract good fortune to those who wore it. Many jewels containing amazonite were found in King Tutankhamen's tomb.

USE FOR

Use this powerful crystal during meditation: it has a deep calming effect on the mind, assisting in the release of negative emotions. Sitting with this stone will help to magnify your intentions while cleansing and purifying the energy around you.

HOME AND SPACE

This is an effective stone for an office or a workspace. As a stone of prosperity, it will attract new customers and positive opportunities to a business. Amazonite will also protect against irritability and allow you to remain focused and balanced throughout the day.

CHAKRA AND BODY

Amazonite is a wonderful stone for energizing both the heart and throat chakras. Known as a stone of truth, it will bring honest and open communication and self-expression to all aspects of life.

LEFT amazonite
RIGHT malachite

Malachite For Personal Transformation

Malachite is a powerful stone of growth and transformation. It enhances spiritual awareness and personal growth. As a stone of protection, malachite guards against negativity of all kinds while attracting abundance and positive energy to all areas of life.

HEALING PROPERTIES

- Growth
- Transformation
- Protection
- Abundance
- Healing

COLOUR AND FORMATION

This crystal is known for its beautiful rich, green colour, often containing lighter or darker bands. It is an opaque stone that is found naturally in raw fibrous formations. Tumbled malachite is the safest variety to use for healing purposes, as it is less friable. Raw malachite can be toxic if ingested in large quantities and must be handled with care.

SOURCE AND HISTORY

Quite a common stone, malachite is found in many countries, including the United States, Chile, Romania, Democratic Republic of the Congo, South Africa, Russia and Australia. It is one of the most ancient stones and has been used for thousands of years for its beauty and healing properties. In ancient Egypt, malachite was seen as a stone of royalty, often worn as a talisman of power and protection.

USE FOR

Used during meditation, this beautiful stone promotes emotional and spiritual transformation and is an effective antidepressant. Malachite will calm the mind and bring a deep sense of peace and harmony.

HOME AND SPACE

Malachite is an effective cleansing crystal and can be kept in the office or workspace to protect against electromagnetic pollution. It also promotes clear thinking and creativity within the workplace.

CHAKRA AND BODY

With its stabilizing energy, malachite assists in aligning all seven chakras. It is especially effective on the heart chakra, facilitating deep emotional healing and promoting harmony in relationships.

TRY THIS Amazonite works wonderfully as an energy filter. Keep it near your computer to protect against electromagnetic pollution. Wear or carry malachite while travelling to overcome a fear of flying and to prevent accidents.

Topaz For Manifestation

Traditionally known as a stone of good fortune, topaz carries an uplifting energy of abundance and joy. It is a powerful amplifier of intention, making it an excellent manifestation stone to attract prosperity and success.

HEALING PROPERTIES

- Abundance
- Manifestation
- Success
- Happiness
- Creativity

COLOUR AND FORMATION

Topaz may be colourless, honey-yellow, brown, gold, pink, green or blue. The crystals are typically transparent and terminated. Topaz is also a popular gemstone to facet into jewellery.

SOURCE AND HISTORY

Topaz is commonly found in the United States, Mexico, India, South Africa, Pakistan and Australia. In Hindu mythology topaz represents long life and intelligence and is a sacred stone of the divine kalpa tree – also known as a wishing tree or tree of life. To the ancient Egyptians, this stone represented the sun god, Ra.

USE FOR

Use this crystal to facilitate meditation: topaz promotes spiritual development and is a powerful stone to enhance visualization and to strengthen intentions. Meditating with this crystal will bring the mind, body and spirit into balance.

HOME AND SPACE

Keep topaz in the office or workspace to inspire creativity and success. This crystal will also increase motivation and confidence.

CHAKRA AND BODY

Depending on the colour, topaz will balance and activate different chakras. Yellow and gold variations work with the solar plexus chakra, encouraging self-esteem, confidence and emotional stability. Blue topaz activates the throat chakra, promoting open communication and self-expression.

TRY THIS Wear topaz on your person to attract abundance, success and joy into your life.

WORKS WELL WITH Pair topaz with citrine (see page 55) to amplify positive energy. This crystal combination will bring a sense of warmth and happiness, while eliminating negative energy from your space.

TRY THIS Use rose quartz in a face mask (see page 171) for a soft, glowing complexion.

WORKS WELL WITH Rose quartz works wonderfully with moonstone (see page 150) to assist with fertility and pregnancy.

Rose Quartz For Unconditional Love

Rose quartz has long been recognized as the stone of unconditional love. With its beautiful soft, pink hue and gentle energy, this stone brings deep inner healing and peace. Rose quartz will help to restore trust in relationships, soothe the heart in times of grief or loss and will encourage self-love and acceptance.

HEALING PROPERTIES

- Love
- Healing
- Peace
- Rejuvenation
- Harmony

COLOUR AND FORMATION

Rose quartz grows as large, rough, translucent pieces in various shades of pink. It is a popular stone to cut and polish for jewellery and other decorative purposes.

SOURCE AND HISTORY

Rose quartz is found in many places around the world, including the United States, Brazil, South Africa, Madagascar and India. Known as a token of love and relationships, the crystal has been revered by many ancient cultures throughout history. The ancient Egyptians and Romans believed it to be a stone of youth and beauty, and used it in facial masks to maintain a clear complexion.

USE FOR

Use rose quartz in a crystal grid (see page 174) to promote healthy relationships of all kinds. This can be effective for attracting new love, creating harmony within an existing relationship or for strengthening bonds within the family.

HOME AND SPACE

This is a beautiful stone to have in the bedroom to create a loving, intimate and restful environment. Keep a small piece under your pillow to encourage a peaceful sleep.

CHAKRA AND BODY

Rose quartz is a crystal for the heart chakra. It can open the heart on all levels, resulting in a clearer understanding of love, compassion and peace.

TRY THIS Wear chrysocolla in a necklace to encourage thoughtful communication, self-awareness and sensitivity.

WORKS WELL WITH Chrysocolla and rose quartz (see page 64) make a powerful combination for healing unstable relationships. Use the two stones together to attract love, compassion and positive energy.

Chrysocolla For Communication

Chrysocolla is widely known as a stone of knowledge and communication. It encourages the expression of feminine energy, teaching the importance of kindness, patience and compassion. This is also a powerful stone for relationships, strengthening the connection between two people and encouraging both men and women to communicate in a positive, loving manner.

HEALING PROPERTIES

- Communication
- Compassion
- Love
- Harmony
- Peace

USE FOR

Used during meditation, chrysocolla attracts positive and loving energies. It will allow you to feel open and connected to yourself and others, leaving you feeling revitalized, empowered and stress-free.

COLOUR AND FORMATION

Chrysocolla is an opaque stone with a beautiful blue-green hue. It is quite porous and soft, growing in large masses rather than in individual crystals.

HOME AND SPACE

This is a wonderful stone for balancing energies within the home. Keep it in a space where you can sit quietly or meditate close by, or in the living room to promote harmony and happiness within the family.

SOURCE AND HISTORY

This stone can be found in the United States, Mexico, Peru, Great Britain, Democratic Republic of the Congo, Russia and Australia. Historically it has seen various applications – not only decorative, but also medicinal. In the late 1800s, for example, chrysocolla was used by European physicians in essences with honey and water for pain relief and to heal sore throats.

CHAKRA AND BODY

Chrysocolla is most often associated with the heart and throat chakras, fostering inner strength, courage and self-expression.

TRY THIS Meditating with chrysoprase will help you to gain a deeper connection with nature and will enhance personal and spiritual growth.

WORKS WELL WITH Chrysoprase and rose quartz (see page 64) make a powerful combination for attracting love and abundance.

Chrysoprase For Trust

A stone of happiness, optimism and love, chrysoprase carries a calming energy that balances the emotions and protects against anxiety and depression. It also promotes forgiveness and trust, helping to strengthen relationships and to attract new love.

HEALING PROPERTIES

- Joy
- Optimism
- Love
- Abundance
- Trust

COLOUR AND FORMATION

This crystal is an opaque or sometimes translucent stone, with a beautiful bright-green hue, often flecked with cream or brown. Chrysoprase forms in relatively small raw pieces that are quite dense, making them a popular gemstone for jewellery and other ornamental objects.

SOURCE AND HISTORY

Found in the United States, Brazil, Tanzania, Madagascar and Australia, chrysoprase has been a popular stone for thousands of years due to its bright and beautiful colour. In ancient Greece, the crystal was believed to be the sacred stone of Aphrodite, the goddess of love.

USE FOR

Wearing chrysoprase is one of the most effective ways to benefit from the crystal's healing properties. It is recognized as being a wonderful support stone for love and relationships, especially for people who struggle with codependency. Chrysoprase will encourage strong commitment without inhibiting independence and self-growth.

HOME AND SPACE

This is a beautiful water-energizing stone: amplify the stone's energies by keeping it in the bathroom or holding it while in the bath. This will create a soothing environment for the relief of stress and anxiety.

CHAKRA AND BODY

Chrysoprase is predominantly a stone of the heart chakra. It will stimulate the flow of loving energy through the heart, attracting abundance and assisting in emotional healing.

Dioptase For Forgiveness

Dioptase is a powerful stone of the heart. Its energy is soothing, bringing focus and stillness to the mind. This crystal encourages a higher state of consciousness and promotes happiness and forgiveness in a relationship. It is also a cleansing crystal, clearing its environment of negativity while attracting love and abundance.

HEALING PROPERTIES
- Compassion
- Forgiveness
- Joy
- Love
- Balance

COLOUR AND FORMATION

Dioptase occurs as small hexagonal crystals that are usually translucent. Its incredibly vibrant colour ranges from blue-green turquoise to emerald green.

SOURCE AND HISTORY

Sources of dioptase exist in Peru, Chile, North Africa, Democratic Republic of the Congo, Namibia, Iran and Russia. The mineral has been valued for its incredible colour for thousands of years. The first known use of the stone dates back to 7200 BC – in the late twentieth century excavations at Ain Ghazal, Jordan, uncovered ancient pre-pottery statues, some of which had eyes decorated in dioptase.

USE FOR

Dioptase has a strong vibration of compassion and forgiveness. It is an effective crystal to use in an unstable relationship. Meditating with this crystal replaces negative energies or thoughts with feelings of love and compassion.

HOME AND SPACE

Dioptase is a lovely stone to keep in the bedroom. It will emit waves of serenity, allowing you to enter a state of peace and tranquility.

CHAKRA AND BODY

With its pure vibration of love and compassion, dioptase will activate and heal the heart chakra. This crystal will align all seven chakras, bringing a sense of harmony, balance and wellbeing.

TRY THIS Use dioptase in a crystal room spray (see page 173) and apply throughout your home as a way of cleansing the space.

WORKS WELL WITH Combine dioptase with chrysocolla (see page 66) if you are working towards a significant change in your life.

Kunzite For New Mums

Known as a 'woman's stone', kunzite carries a pure loving energy that radiates peace and harmony. Promoting unconditional love and happiness, it is perfect for new mothers or during pregnancy. As kunzite contains lithium, it amplifies positive energies, encouraging emotional balance and eliminating negative thought patterns.

HEALING PROPERTIES

- Love
- Peace
- Joy
- Patience
- Harmony

COLOUR AND FORMATION

Most often, kunzite forms as prismatic crystals that are transparent or translucent with soft pink, lilac or green colouring.

SOURCE AND HISTORY

A relatively new stone, kunzite was discovered in 1902. Since that time, sources have been found in the United States, Brazil, Madagascar, Afghanistan and Myanmar.

USE FOR

Known as a 'guardian crystal', kunzite is said to aid communication with spirit guides.

Holding this stone during meditation will enhance your intuition and deepen your meditative state. The stone is especially helpful to those who are just learning to meditate, or who struggle to remain centred.

HOME AND SPACE

Keep kunzite in a baby's nursery or in your own bedroom to promote a peaceful and restful environment. This is also an effective stone for young children who have trouble sleeping.

CHAKRA AND BODY

Kunzite is closely associated with the heart and crown chakras, enhancing open communication, balance and mental clarity.

> **TRY THIS** Place ruby in the abundance/prosperity corner of your home (see page 32) to attract abundance and good fortune.
> Wear kunzite to promote emotional healing and forgiveness in a relationship.

Ruby For Passion

Ruby is primarily recognized as a symbol of passion and vitality. It is an excellent stone for increasing energy and motivation when feeling lethargic, and can bring a new sense of enthusiasm for life. Ruby is also a powerful stone for attracting love and good fortune, and will help restore a relationship that has become unstable.

HEALING PROPERTIES

- Passion
- Vitality
- Energy
- Motivation
- Love

COLOUR AND FORMATION

This crystal can be found in varying shades of red, often growing in prismatic formations or in masses. Rubies occur as opaque or transparent crystals, with transparency regarded as a mark of higher quality.

SOURCE AND HISTORY

Ruby can be found in the United States, Mexico, Cambodia, Madagascar, India, Russia and Sri Lanka. Among many cultures, particularly in Asia, it has been known as a symbol of love and royalty. Historically, ruby was carried as a talisman of protection and good fortune. In the ancient Indian language of Sanskrit, ruby is known as 'ratnaraj', meaning 'king of precious stones'.

USE FOR

Wearing this stone will boost your energy levels and will enhance self-confidence and inner power. Ruby is also a wonderful stone to wear for maintaining healthy relationships, as it strengthens commitment, love, trust and emotional stability.

HOME AND SPACE

This stone will remove stress and will prevent you feeling emotionally disconnected from yourself or others. Keep ruby in the bedroom to promote closeness and intimacy or to attract new love.

CHAKRA AND BODY

Ruby energizes the root chakra, encouraging balance, strength and passion.

Opal For Commitment

Opal is a stone of happiness and purity. It is associated with love and passion, enhancing commitment and loyalty in relationships. This delicate stone has a light and loving energy that is believed to attract good luck and abundance.

HEALING PROPERTIES

- Love
- Passion
- Happiness
- Purity
- Commitment

USE FOR

Wearing opal is a beautiful way of benefiting from the many healing properties of the stone. It brings lightheartedness and happiness to the wearer while enhancing courage and self-confidence.

COLOUR AND FORMATION

Opal may appear in a wide variety of colours including pink, yellow, orange, green, purple or red. These beautiful stones often form in masses or in veins. They are often small and translucent with bright iridescent flashes.

SOURCE AND HISTORY

Opal can be found in Canada, the United States, Mexico, Peru, Great Britain and Australia. The stone carries a rich and wonderful history of many ancient mythologies. In ancient Rome, opal was believed to carry the power of all other gemstones as it displayed the vibrant colours of each of them.

HOME AND SPACE

Keep opal in the bedroom to enhance passion, and to bring new vitality and spontaneity into a relationship. This stone will also strengthen the bond between two people by encouraging kindness, love and compassion.

CHAKRA AND BODY

Opal resonates strongly with the sacral and root chakras, enhancing passion and creativity while bringing stability to the mind and emotions.

TRY THIS Meditate with opal to amplify your intentions and to assist in releasing any negative thoughts or emotions.

WORKS WELL WITH Opal and kunzite (see page 72) make a beautiful combination for attracting love and happiness.

Emerald For Successful Love

This powerful crystal has a wide range of healing properties. Known as the 'stone of successful love', it brings new energy and vitality to a relationship while inspiring passion, commitment and trust. Emerald teaches generosity and kindness, making it a wonderful tool not only to strengthen romantic relationships, but also to improve connections with family members and friends.

HEALING PROPERTIES

- Joy
- Communication
- Compassion
- Peace
- Intuition

COLOUR AND FORMATION

A variety of beryl, emerald forms beautiful green, hexagonal crystals that may be opaque or transparent depending on their quality. Generally, the more transparent an emerald is, the more highly it is prized.

SOURCE AND HISTORY

Emerald can be found in Colombia, Brazil, Tanzania, Egypt, Pakistan, India and Australia. It is one of the most valued stones in history and has been used across many cultures for more than 5,000 years. In Europe, during the Middle Ages, it was thought that emerald was a revealer of truth and that it would protect its wearer against spells and enchantments. In ancient Egypt, this stone was considered to represent eternal life.

USE FOR

This is an effective stone for instilling patience. Use emerald to calm the mind and emotions during meditation, and to achieve a state of tranquility and self-awareness. The crystal will allow you to focus your intention and will encourage you to remain emotionally present.

HOME AND SPACE

Kept in the office or workspace, emerald will enhance focus and mental clarity. The stone will also promote success, creativity and inspiration while cleansing the area of any negative or stagnant energy.

CHAKRA AND BODY

Emerald is a stone that activates the heart chakra, encouraging compassion, peace and emotional healing.

Hemimorphite For Empathy

Hemimorphite holds a sweet and calming energy that attracts joy, happiness and positivity. This stone is excellent for maintaining healthy relationships, as it encourages open communication, empathy and understanding between two people.

HEALING PROPERTIES
- Joy
- Positivity
- Empathy
- Communication
- Compassion

COLOUR AND FORMATION
Usually opaque or translucent, this beautiful stone is most often found in various shades of blue, green or white that also may also contain areas of darker tone.

SOURCE AND HISTORY
Hemimorphite is found all over the world, including the United States, Mexico, Italy, Greece, South Africa, Madagascar and Australia. Initially, it was confused with a mineral now known as smithsonite. Both stones were collectively called calamine before the 1800s, after which it was discovered that they were, in fact, separate minerals.

USE FOR
Wear or carry hemimorphite when you are struggling with a relationship. Although a very useful stone for couples, it can also be helpful in restoring relationships with friends and family members. Hemimorphite encourages forgiveness, patience and understanding, and allows unstable relationships to heal.

HOME AND SPACE
Keeping hemimorphite in the social areas of the home, such as the living room or kitchen, will help balance family dynamics and will promote happy, loving relationships.

CHAKRA AND BODY
Hemimorphite resonates well with the heart and throat chakras, promoting emotional healing and open communication. It is also connected to the third eye chakra and will assist in heightening spiritual awareness and intuition.

> **TRY THIS** Place emerald in the abundance/ prosperity corner of your home (see page 32) to attract abundance, wealth and prosperity. Place hemimorphite in a crystal grid (see page 174) to manifest good fortune, joy and wellbeing on all levels.

Rhodonite For Love and Protection

Known as a crystal of love and protection, rhodonite carries a joyful vibration that brings happiness, forgiveness and peace. It promotes emotional stability and provides relief from anxiety and depression.

HEALING PROPERTIES

- Love
- Happiness
- Stability
- Peace
- Healing

COLOUR AND FORMATION

Rhodonite is a pink stone that varies from light rose to deep magenta, often containing black inclusions. It is commonly formed in great masses that are usually opaque.

SOURCE AND HISTORY

The crystal is found in many places, including Canada, the United States, Mexico, Brazil, Germany, India, Russia and Australia. Originally found in Russia in the 1700s, rhodonite became a popular stone that was carried as a talisman of protection. It was also called the 'eagle stone' as eagles would be seen taking small pieces of rhodonite to their nests. Soon after, it became a tradition for the locals to place rhodonite stones in their babies' cribs as a symbol of love, strength and protection.

USE FOR

This is an effective stone to carry during traumatic or stressful times. Its nurturing energy heals emotional shock and will help you through times of grief or loss.

HOME AND SPACE

Place rhodonite in the centre of the home to balance the feminine and masculine energies, and to create a positive energy flow throughout the house.

CHAKRA AND BODY

Rhodonite is most commonly associated with the heart chakra promoting peace, balance and compassion.

Sugilite For Emotional Support

Sugilite is known as a 'stone of love', facilitating emotional healing and spiritual transformation. It carries a highly supportive energy, helping to alleviate feelings of grief, fear or loss. Emotionally, sugilite promotes inner strength, peace and stability.

HEALING PROPERTIES

- Love
- Healing
- Growth
- Stability
- Peace

COLOUR AND FORMATION

Sugilite is most often found as a rough opaque stone with beautiful shades of pink and purple. Although it is usually granular (grainy), in some rare cases it can form small prismatic crystals.

SOURCE AND HISTORY

Not discovered until the 1940s, sugilite is a very new addition to the world of crystals. It is found in Canada, South Africa and Japan. It is quickly becoming a popular stone for energy healers.

USE FOR

Wear or carry sugilite to instil peace and relaxation. The stone brings a sense of comfort and stability and is effective in alleviating stress and anxiety. A highly nurturing stone, sugilite encourages physical and emotional healing while protecting against negative energy.

HOME AND SPACE

Sugilite encourages harmony and forgiveness within the home, helping to create a loving space of unity and support within the family. Keep the stone in the living areas of the home to attract positivity, warmth and brightness.

CHAKRA AND BODY

This a stone that will balance and align all seven chakras, particularly the crown and third eye. As a stone of healing and spiritual development, sugilite heightens intuition and brings clarity to the mind and emotions.

TRY THIS Place sugilite in a crystal grid (see page 174) to protect against negative energy and to attract love, happiness and healing.

WORKS WELL WITH Paired with rose quartz (see page 64) sugilite brings stability, love and connection to a relationship.

Lodolite Quartz For Inner Strength

Also known as 'garden quartz', lodolite quartz contains a powerful, yet grounding, energy. The stone encourages inner strength and attracts loving vibrations into your life. The clear quartz element of this crystal increases the vibrations of its inclusions, making it a wonderful amplifier of energy.

HEALING PROPERTIES

- Abundance
- Power
- Inner strength
- Transformation
- Healing

COLOUR AND FORMATION

This variety of quartz contains various minerals, including feldspar, hematite and chlorite, among others. These elements bring different colours of green, brown, red or cream that often create a unique garden or landscape effect within the crystal.

SOURCE AND HISTORY

Lodolite quartz is found mainly in Brazil. The stones are known to promote a deep connection with nature and shamans, or spiritual healers, have used lodolite quartz throughout history as a way of inducing healing experiences and visions.

USE FOR

This is a powerful stone to use when setting intentions or to help manifest abundance in your life. Hold a crystal during meditation to strengthen spiritual awareness and to attract positivity and joy. Lodolite quartz will also encourage you to let go of past life attachments or break out of old patterns.

HOME AND SPACE

The energy of lodolite quartz is traditionally associated with the family rooms of the home. Keeping this crystal in the living room will promote harmonious relationships with family members and friends.

CHAKRA AND BODY

While lodolite quartz has the ability to clear all of the chakras, it is primarily associated with the crown chakra. Placing this stone at the top of your head will bring clarity to the mind and emotions while helping to cleanse any negative energy.

TRY THIS Place lodolite quartz by your bed for vivid dreams and heightened spiritual awareness.

WORKS WELL WITH Lodolite quartz works beautifully with scolecite (see page 130) to facilitate deep inner healing and spiritual transformation.

TRY THIS For pain relief, place a lapis lazuli crystal over the affected area to alleviate symptoms.

WORKS WELL WITH Pair lapis lazuli with amethyst (see page 122) to promote emotional, spiritual and physical healing.

Lapis Lazuli For Intuition

Lapis lazuli is one of the most sought-after stones in history. It has extremely powerful healing properties and is often recognized as a symbol of honour and royalty. Lapis lazuli is a powerful thought amplifier, enhancing psychic abilities and intuition. It is also said to release feelings of frustration and anger.

HEALING PROPERTIES

- Power
- Intuition
- Prosperity
- Truth
- Wisdom

COLOUR AND FORMATION

A deep-blue opaque stone formed as a rough mass, lapis lazuli is often flecked with white calcite or golden pyrite.

SOURCE AND HISTORY

This crystal is found in the United States, the Middle East, Egypt, Afghanistan and Russia. In ancient Egypt, amulets were carved from lapis lazuli and worn as symbols of great power and wisdom. Due to its brilliant blue colour, the crystal was also ground down by the Egyptians to use for paint and dyes.

USE FOR

Using lapis lazuli will help you remain focused while increasing your concentration and clearing your mind of any stress. Wear this crystal to enhance your intuition and intellect.

HOME AND SPACE

With its soothing energy, lapis lazuli is an effective stone for sleep. Keeping a piece in the bedroom will create a more peaceful space and will allow your body to relax and fully recharge overnight.

CHAKRA AND BODY

Lapis lazuli activates the third eye and throat chakras. It stimulates spiritual enlightenment and will bring deep inner peace during meditation. It will also encourage open communication and remove the fear of public speaking.

Aventurine For Personal Growth

Aventurine is a stone of health, wellbeing and happiness. It encourages personal growth and facilitates the release of unhealthy attachments or relationships. Aventurine also reduces feelings of stress and anxiety, while bringing a deep sense of comfort and inner peace.

HEALING PROPERTIES

- Happiness
- Personal growth
- Healing
- Positivity
- Renewal

COLOUR AND FORMATION

Though aventurine is widely recognized for its beautiful green colour, it may also form in yellow, blue and orange hues. Stones are usually translucent or opaque and may be speckled with a light shimmer.

SOURCE AND HISTORY

Aventurine is found in Brazil, Italy, India, Russia, China and Nepal. It has been used for thousands of years for its healing properties and prized for its beautiful colour. Historically, green aventurine was used in China to decorate the eyes of statues to bring visionary powers.

USE FOR

Wearing aventurine is an effective way to attract positivity into your life. Its soothing energy will allow you to feel happy, confident and clear-headed throughout the day. Wearing aventurine will also protect against electromagnetic and environmental pollutants.

HOME AND SPACE

Keep aventurine in family areas of the home such as the kitchen or living room, to encourage physical and emotional health and wellbeing. The stone also carries a nurturing energy that is beneficial for young children.

CHAKRA AND BODY

Aventurine is associated primarily with the heart chakra. It is a comforting stone that will attract love, healing and forgiveness to one's life.

TRY THIS Use green aventurine in an essence (see page 172) to calm nervousness, stress or irritability.

WORKS WELL WITH Paired with moonstone (see page 150) aventurine balances the masculine and feminine energies within the home (see page 32).

Apophyllite For Calm

Apophyllite is a high-vibration crystal that contains a very uplifting energy. Calming and balancing, it will help overcome feelings of anxiety, stress and fear. This is a powerful crystal for the mind and emotions, as it releases mental blockages and removes negative thought patterns.

HEALING PROPERTIES

- Intuition
- Spirituality
- Enlightenment
- Wellness
- Positivity

COLOUR AND FORMATION

Apophyllite appears as either cubic or pyramidal crystals that may be opaque, translucent or completely clear. Occurring in a range of colours, crystals can be found in shades of peach, green, yellow, grey or white.

SOURCE AND HISTORY

This crystal is commonly found in the United States, Brazil, Greenland, Iceland, Germany, Italy, India and Australia. It was discovered in the early 1800s and has since become widely collected for its beauty as well as its metaphysical properties.

USE FOR

Using this very powerful stone during meditation will allow you to connect to spiritual realms. It will enhance mental clarity and intuition, allowing you to focus your energy and intention while expanding your inner vision.

HOME AND SPACE

Place apophyllite in the social rooms of the home, such as the living room or kitchen, where it will remove negative energies and replace them with uplifting vibrations of peace, love and happiness.

CHAKRA AND BODY

Depending on the colour of the stone, apophyllite can work with different chakras. For example, green apophyllite will focus more upon the heart chakra, bringing emotional healing and support. Meanwhile white apophyllite activates the third eye chakra, strengthening intuition and promoting spiritual awareness.

TRY THIS Use this crystal in a grid (see page 174), to purify the space and to invite light and loving energy.

WORKS WELL WITH Pair apophyllite with clear quartz (see page 104) to enhance intuition and to promote positive energy flow.

TRY THIS Meditate with angelite to
assist personal or spiritual growth. Wear
rhodochrosite in a necklace to encourage self-
acceptance and to soothe emotional stress.

Angelite For Spiritual Awareness

Angelite is considered to be one of the most powerful stones for
enhancing spiritual awareness. As its name suggests, it is associated
with the energies of the angelic realm. Its vibration is incredibly
potent and can help you to discover your own sense of spirituality.

HEALING PROPERTIES
- Spirituality
- Understanding
- Peace
- Wellness
- Intuition

COLOUR AND FORMATION
Angelite is a fragile blue stone, often veined
or flecked with white. It may also be referred
to as blue anhydrite and is formed as a result
of gypsum losing its water content. Its name
is derived from the Greek word *anhydrous*
meaning 'without water'.

SOURCE AND HISTORY
This crystal is found in Mexico, Peru,
Great Britain, Germany, Poland and Egypt.
Discovered as recently as the 1980s in Peru,
angelite has quickly become a favourite
among crystal healers today.

USE FOR
Carrying energies of peace, compassion
and understanding, angelite is a beautiful
stone with which to meditate. It promotes a
deep sense of tranquility and can be used as
a talisman to connect with spirit guides.

HOME AND SPACE
Calming and comforting, angelite is the
perfect stone to keep in the bedroom. It will
help to soothe an overactive mind and can
protect against insomnia.

CHAKRA AND BODY
Angelite will activate the throat, third
eye and crown chakras, encouraging clear
communication and enhanced intuition.

Rhodochrosite For Emotional Healing

This stone clears negative energy, encourages personal growth and balances the nervous system, making it a wonderful tool for emotional healing. Extremely desirable due to its beautiful colour and powerful healing abilities, rhodochrosite is also a stone of compassion and unconditional love.

HEALING PROPERTIES

- Healing
- Positivity
- Transformation
- Compassion
- Love

COLOUR AND FORMATION

This beautiful stone forms in a variety of interesting ways; it may be seen as opaque banded slabs, sparkling clusters or in perfect transparent cubes. Whatever its shape, rhodochrosite is widely recognized for its vibrant shades of pink.

SOURCE AND HISTORY

Primarily sourced from Argentina, rhodochrosite can also be found in the United States, Uruguay, South Africa and Russia. It is thought to have been discovered in the thirteenth century by an Incan ruler who named the stone 'Inca rose'. The Incans believed that these crystals were sacred and carried the blood of their ancestral rulers.

USE FOR

Rhodochrosite carries a light and loving vibration that allows you to confront your fears and rid yourself of negative patterns or people in your life. Use this stone during meditation to bring these emotions gently to the surface so that you can release them, heal and move on.

HOME AND SPACE

Place rhodochrosite in a bedroom to create a nurturing and peaceful environment. This stone will encourage passion in an existing relationship or will assist in attracting new love. It will also bring subtle energies of commitment, companionship and affection.

CHAKRA AND BODY

This crystal is known as a stone for the solar plexus chakra, manifesting joy, happiness and abundance in one's life. It also activates the heart chakra; promoting unconditional love and the acceptance of oneself, rhodochrosite fosters love and forgiveness on all levels.

LEFT angelite
RIGHT rhodochrosite

Blue Lace Agate For Peace

Blue lace agate carries a calming vibration that attracts peace and harmony to all areas of life. It is a beautiful healing stone, promoting emotional stability, confidence and mental clarity.

HEALING PROPERTIES

- Peace
- Harmony
- Stability
- Confidence
- Expression

COLOUR AND FORMATION

Blue lace agate displays beautiful soft blue and white hues. It can also be recognized by its unique banded stripes and patterns. Like most types of agate, this stone forms as layered nodules in volcanic rocks. Its strength and durability makes it a popular stone to cut and polish into jewellery or display pieces.

SOURCE AND HISTORY

Blue lace agate is found in the United States, Mexico, Brazil, Morocco, Namibia and India. It was discovered in the 1960s and has since become a popular stone due to its beautiful appearance as well as its calming and uplifting energies.

USE FOR

This is a beautiful stone to meditate with, due to its peaceful vibration. This crystal will encourage physical and emotional healing while promoting inner stability and relaxation.

HOME AND SPACE

A beautiful water-energizing stone, blue lace agate works well in the bathroom. Place it by the sink or hold it while in the bath. This will create a soothing environment while amplifying the stone's natural healing energies of peace and tranquillity.

CHAKRA AND BODY

Blue lace agate is primarily associated with the throat chakra, encouraging self-expression and communication.

TRY THIS Use blue lace agate in an essence (see page 172) to relieve stress and calm the mind.

WORKS WELL WITH Combined with amethyst (see page 122), blue lace agate will infuse your space with tranquil and serene energies.

Shungite For Balance

Shungite is regarded as one of the strongest healing minerals on the planet. Often referred to as the 'stone of life', shungite restores emotional, spiritual and physical balance. It is a stone of many wonderful properties, bringing emotional stability, vitality and overall wellbeing.

HEALING PROPERTIES

- Healing
- Balance
- Purity
- Wellness
- Vitality

COLOUR AND FORMATION

This opaque, black stone often has a shiny metallic surface. Shungite forms in non-crystalline structures that consist of over 90 per cent carbon, as well as fullerenes – powerful antioxidants.

SOURCE AND HISTORY

Primarily found in Russia, shungite is a powerful ancient stone, believed to be more than two billion years old. Since its discovery in the 1700s, it has been used in Russia for its water-purifying qualities. The first Russian spa established in 1719 by Peter the Great, used the purifying qualities of shungite to cleanse the spring water so people could bathe in it.

USE FOR

Use this powerful stone in an essence (see page 172). Simply by placing the stone in water and allowing it to sit for a short time, the water becomes purified and charged with a potent healing vibration. It is believed that drinking this essence will detoxify the body and may even promote an increased rate of cellular growth and rejuvenation.

HOME AND SPACE

Keep shungite in the bathroom to use as a part of your beauty routine. The stone is known to contain many benefits for the skin and can be used in cleansing water for maintaining a clear and youthful complexion.

CHAKRA AND BODY

Shungite cleanses and balances all seven chakras, but is most closely associated with the root chakra, bringing a strong sense of stability, energy and vitality.

LEFT shungite
RIGHT moldavite

Moldavite For Inner Healing

A rare and powerful stone, moldavite carries an intense energy of inner healing and transformation. It accelerates spiritual growth and raises consciousness, creating positive changes in all areas of life. Moldavite also raises the vibrations of other stones in its environment, making it a powerful tool to enhance physical, emotional and spiritual wellbeing.

HEALING PROPERTIES

- Energy
- Healing
- Transformation
- Spirituality
- Protection

USE FOR

Use moldavite during meditation to enhance spiritual awareness and transformation. This stone will assist in developing psychic abilities and intuition, encouraging a deep and powerful experience.

COLOUR AND FORMATION

This beautiful glass-like, olive-green stone is often found in small transparent pieces with unique etchings and markings that are the result of millions of years of natural erosion.

SOURCE AND HISTORY

Moldavite is a type of natural glass known as tektite and is found in the Czech Republic. It is believed to have formed during the impact of a meteorite colliding with Earth approximately 14.8 million years ago. In ancient times, moldavite was considered a mystical stone and was carried as a talisman of harmony and good luck in Czechoslovakian folklore. Today, it is believed by many crystal healers to contain extraterrestrial energies.

HOME AND SPACE

Moldavite is most associated with the family areas of the home. Keep it in the dining room or kitchen to increase health and vitality. As a stone of growth and renewal, moldavite will also aid in the nurturing, development and growth of young children.

CHAKRA AND BODY

This crystal is primarily associated with the crown, third eye and heart chakras. It will bring insight and guidance to your own understanding of spirituality.

TRY THIS Use shungite in a cleansing water for a healthy glowing complexion. Carry or wear moldavite to amplify its effects and to protect against negative energy entering your space.

TRY THIS Place fuchsite in a crystal grid (see page 174) to attract happiness and wellbeing into your home.

WORKS WELL WITH Combined with lepidolite (see page 128), fuchsite will enhance love, joy and emotional healing.

Fuchsite For Healing

Known as the 'healer's stone', fuchsite carries strong healing vibrations of strength and wellness. The crystal releases energy blockages and encourages resilience during times of stress.

HEALING PROPERTIES

- Healing
- Resilience
- Wellness
- Joy
- Rejuvenation

COLOUR AND FORMATION

Fuchsite appears as opaque layers and can be found in shimmering shades of green, often with a brilliant sparkle.

SOURCE AND HISTORY

This crystal is found in Brazil, Zimbabwe, India and Russia. In African-Brazillian tradition, it was considered to be a gift from the sea goddess, Lemanja.

USE FOR

Wearing or carrying this beautiful stone with you will help you make the most of its healing benefits. Fuchsite will encourage you to feel physically and emotionally balanced while attracting happiness and contentment to all areas of your life.

HOME AND SPACE

Keep fuchsite in the bedroom to encourage relaxation and deep sleep. Keeping this stone under your pillow will allow you to wake up feeling content, happy and refreshed.

CHAKRA AND BODY

Fuchsite is primarily a heart chakra stone, promoting light-heartedness and compassion.

TRY THIS Use danburite in a crystal room spray (see page 173) to detoxify and cleanse your home of any negative energies.

WORKS WELL WITH Danburite works beautifully with kunzite (see page 72) to attract unconditional love and healing.

Danburite For Inner Guidance

Danburite carries an uplifting energy that assists in emotional healing and alleviates feelings of stress and anxiety. It is also a stone of wisdom and inner guidance. It will promote a higher state of consciousness and enhanced intuition.

HEALING PROPERTIES

- Balance
- Healing
- Enlightenment
- Love
- Harmony

COLOUR AND FORMATION

Danburite crystals are prismatic in shape and are usually transparent or translucent. They may be colourless or contain pastel hues of pink or yellow.

SOURCE AND HISTORY

Discovered in 1839, this crystal was found in Danbury, Connecticut, in the United States, and was named danburite after the city. Today the stone is also found in Mexico, Russia, Myanmar and Japan.

USE FOR

Danburite is a good stone to use during meditation, especially if you suffer from anxiety. The stone will relax your mind and encourage a deep meditative state. If you are going through emotional changes, danburite will facilitate the process while promoting feelings of self-love and acceptance.

HOME AND SPACE

Keep danburite in the bedroom to attract positive energy into the space. If you struggle with insomnia, this stone will soothe the mind, heart and emotions, allowing you to feel grounded and centred.

CHAKRA AND BODY

Spiritually, danburite opens the third eye and crown chakras, promoting harmony, awareness and intuition. This crystal also activates the heart chakra, encouraging heartfelt expression, forgiveness and self-love.

TRY THIS Create a crystal grid (see page 174) in your home using lithium quartz. This will bring harmony and balance to your living space and to family dynamics and relationships.

WORKS WELL WITH Lithium quartz works powerfully with rose quartz (see page 64) to create a strong heart-healing combination. Use these stones together to release ties from negative relationships or during times of grief or loss.

Lithium Quartz For Tranquility

Lithium quartz is popular for its strong metaphysical properties. Known as a natural antidepressant, it contains a sweet and calming energy that releases tension and eliminates fear, anxiety and depression. This stone is a gentle healer that encourages happiness and emotional peace, restoring harmony and balance to one's life.

HEALING PROPERTIES

- Healing
- Balance
- Harmony
- Peace
- Tranquility

COLOUR AND FORMATION

A combination of clear quartz with purple, pink or grey lithium inclusions, lithium quartz forms naturally in translucent or opaque points and clusters.

SOURCE AND HISTORY

Only found in Brazil, for many years this crystal has been a symbol of luxury, intuition and spirituality. Lithium quartz is also considered to be a 'guardian crystal', known to help protect a person and their family against harm, as well as their home and valuables.

USE FOR

Use lithium quartz for meditation and self-healing. This stone can bring suppressed emotions to the surface gently, allowing you to acknowledge and release any negative attachments or past traumas.

HOME AND SPACE

Keeping lithium quartz in the bedroom will help you feel relaxed and centred before going to bed. Sleeping with a stone under the pillow facilitates deep sleep for both children and adults.

CHAKRA AND BODY

Lithium quartz is a heart-healing crystal and is effective in activating the heart chakra. As an aid to meditation, this crystal will also work with the third eye chakra to deepen meditation practices and keep the mind free of distraction.

Fluorite For Focus

Fluorite carries a calming and stabilizing energy that promotes mental clarity and focus. Regarded as a stone of success and achievement, fluorite encourages deep concentration, allowing the absorption of new information and the flow of creative ideas. It also removes chaotic energies from its environment, making it a wonderful stone for students.

HEALING PROPERTIES

- Focus
- Concentration
- Clarity
- Success
- Stability

COLOUR AND FORMATION

This crystal grows in an incredible cubic formation that is often transparent and may contain subtle etchings or markings on the surface. Vibrant in colour, it is often a brilliant shade of green or purple, however other hues such as pink, blue, yellow or red can also occur.

SOURCE AND HISTORY

Fluorite can be found in the United States, Mexico, Peru, Great Britain, Germany and China. In ancient history, it was seen widely as an ornamental stone and was often carved into amulets, statues and decorative art. In the eighteenth century, powdered fluorite mixed with water was used to relieve kidney disease.

USE FOR

Use fluorite as a tool for remaining organized and focused. Holding a crystal when you are feeling overwhelmed or stressed will help keep the mind clear and calm throughout the day.

HOME AND SPACE

Keep fluorite in the office – close to your computer, where it will be extremely effective against electromagnetic stress. It will cleanse and purify the workspace, encouraging clear thinking and improved concentration.

CHAKRA AND BODY

Purple fluorite energizes the third eye chakra, enhancing intuition, wisdom and spirituality. Green fluorite restores the heart chakra, soothing emotional trauma and opening the heart, while balancing the mind and emotions.

TRY THIS Carry or wear a clear quartz crystal to protect against negative energy and to assist in manifesting your intentions.

WORKS WELL WITH Clear quartz is an amplifier for all other stones and can be paired with any crystal that you wish to amplify.

Clear Quartz For Energy

Clear Quartz is regarded as the most powerful energy amplifier on the planet. It is considered a master healer with a high vibration of positivity. It is the most versatile stone used in crystal healing and can have almost any application, which makes it a highly valued stone by many.

HEALING PROPERTIES
- Energy
- Inspiration
- Power
- Healing
- Manifestation

COLOUR AND FORMATION
Quartz grows as beautiful transparent, or translucent, pointed crystals of any size and shape. Quartz crystals are also often found in clusters.

SOURCE AND HISTORY
Found on almost every continent, quartz is one of the most abundant minerals in the world. For thousands of years, this crystal has been revered as a great source of power in almost every culture. In ancient Rome, it was believed that quartz crystals were solidified water and they were carried for their cooling properties during the summer months.

USE FOR
This is the ideal crystal to use when making grids (see page 174). Place one of these stones in each corner of the home to prevent negative energies entering your space.

HOME AND SPACE
Clear quartz can be kept in any room of the house. It will amplify the energy throughout the home, emitting a loving and healing vibration to all those in its vicinity.

CHAKRA AND BODY
Closely associated with the crown chakra, clear quartz promotes personal growth and spiritual awareness.

Sodalite For Intellectual Stimulation

Sodalite is a wonderful stone for the mind. It assists in strengthening intellect, eliminating confusion and balancing emotions. It carries a calm and stable energy that increases consciousness and deepens meditation. This lovely stone is also effective for enhancing inspiration and creativity.

HEALING PROPERTIES
- Intuition
- Intelligence
- Creativity
- Inspiration
- Focus

USE FOR
Using sodalite during meditation will help calm the mind and eliminate distraction. It will bring a deeper sense of spiritual understanding, allowing you to develop your intuition.

COLOUR AND FORMATION
This stone is recognized by its shade of royal blue, often opaque and veined with white calcite. Other colours may include orange, pink, green and yellow. Sodalite usually forms as a rough mass with a vitreous lustre.

HOME AND SPACE
Keep sodalite in the office or workspace – particularly near your computer – to protect against electromagnetic pollution. This stone will also enhance creativity and focus, making it an excellent choice for creative individuals.

SOURCE AND HISTORY
Sodalite is most often found in the United States, Canada, Brazil, Greenland, Romania and Russia. It was first discovered in Greenland in 1811 and gained further recognition after large deposits were found in Ontario, Canada in 1891. One of the most noteworthy sources is known as the Princess Sodalite mine, named in 1901 after the then Princess of Wales (later Queen Mary, wife of King George V). She was so captivated by the beauty of the stone that, in 1906, 130 tons of sodalite were shipped to England to decorate her London residence, Marlborough House.

CHAKRA AND BODY
Sodalite energizes the throat chakra, encouraging open communication, truthfulness and positive self-expression.

LEFT sodalite
RIGHT calcite

Calcite For Positive Energy

A powerful energy amplifier, calcite eliminates stagnant or negative energy from its environment. The stone encourages higher awareness and spiritual growth, making it a strong tool for emotional healing and development.

HEALING PROPERTIES

- Energy
- Healing
- Motivation
- Vitality
- Confidence

COLOUR AND FORMATION

Calcite appears in a variety of different shapes and forms that may be transparent or opaque. It can take on almost any colour: blue, green, yellow, brown, orange, red, pink or white.

SOURCE AND HISTORY

Calcite is one of the most abundant crystals on Earth and is found in many locations, including the United States, Mexico, Peru, Brazil, Iceland, Great Britain, Belgium and Romania. The ancient Egyptians believed that calcite cleansed energy blockages in the body and used it to adorn the tombs of pharaohs.

USE FOR

Keeping this stone with you throughout the day will alleviate stress and enhance motivation and energy. Calcite will also aid in communication and bring inspiration to those feeling creatively blocked.

HOME AND SPACE

Wherever it is kept, calcite will cleanse, purify and energize the space. A piece in the office will bring abundance and good fortune; placing it in a bedroom will bring peace and tranquility.

CHAKRA AND BODY

Calcite activates all seven chakras, depending on which variation you use. Clear or white calcite, for example, activates the crown chakra, bringing spiritual awareness and higher consciousness. Orange calcite is associated with the root and sacral chakras, and brings balance, creativity and passion.

Jasper For Grounding Energy

With a grounding and peaceful energy, jasper is a very nurturing stone. Harnessing balance and unity, it is effective in reducing stress and anxiety. Considered a stone of vitality, jasper also increases energy and encourages willpower and self-confidence.

HEALING PROPERTIES

- Balance
- Confidence
- Energy
- Vitality
- Courage

COLOUR AND FORMATION

This opaque stone appears in a variety of different colours, often with unique patterns and markings. Its earthy tones can vary from blue, green and yellow through red, white, pink or brown.

SOURCE AND HISTORY

Jasper is found all around the world, but is especially common in India and Australia. Historically, it has been seen as an important stone in many cultures and religions. Considered a symbol of Mother Earth, it was used by Native American shamans for its healing properties to enhance strength, energy and vitality.

USE FOR

Wear jasper to increase mental clarity and to protect against negative energy. This stone will help you to remain grounded and centred while promoting self-confidence and courage. Jasper also brings a strong sense of stability and security during times of stress.

HOME AND SPACE

This is a powerful stone for any area of the home. Placing a piece in a bedroom will promote happiness, passion and harmony in relationships. Used in an office or workspace, jasper will bring energy, motivation and inspiration.

CHAKRA AND BODY

All varieties of jasper carry the grounding and stabilizing energies of the Earth, making it an effective stone for activating the root chakra.

TRY THIS Meditate with jasper to facilitate deep inner peace, and to amplify your intentions.

WORKS WELL WITH Jasper and carnelian (see page 116) make a powerful combination for enhancing passion, creativity and vitality.

TRY THIS Use Herkimer diamonds in a crystal grid (see page 174) to attract positivity, light and healing into your space.

WORKS WELL WITH Pair a Herkimer diamond with kunzite (see page 72) to create a light and loving space for personal development and spiritual transformation.

Herkimer Diamond For Uplifting Energy

Herkimer diamonds are beautiful, high-vibrational crystals that carry an uplifting and spiritual energy. They are known for their powerful cleansing and purifying abilities and are effective stones for protection against negative energy.

HEALING PROPERTIES

- Spirituality
- Purity
- Clarity
- Intuition
- Energy

COLOUR AND FORMATION

A Herkimer diamond is a rare variety of natural, double-terminated quartz – this means that the crystal has a naturally faceted point at each end. Herkimer diamonds may be translucent with a smoky hue, or perfectly clear with stunning clarity and sparkle.

SOURCE AND HISTORY

Predominately found in the United States, Herkimer diamonds have also been discovered in Canada, Mexico, Norway, Spain and China. The crystal acquired its name from the place in which it was first discovered – a small town called Little Falls in Herkimer County, New York.

USE FOR

Herkimer diamonds carry a highly spiritual vibration and offer a wonderful aid to meditation. Stones heighten intuition and are known to amplify spiritual energy. It is an excellent crystal for healing emotional trauma and can be especially helpful to use during difficult times.

HOME AND SPACE

Keep a Herkimer diamond in the bedroom or somewhere that you feel most at ease. Sleeping with a piece nearby will keep your energy field free of impurities while filling the space with light and uplifting energy. Herkimer diamonds are also known to promote lucid dreaming.

CHAKRA AND BODY

Herkimer diamonds are primarily associated with the third eye and crown chakras, through which they encourage spiritual advancement and emotional healing.

Vanadinite For Vitality

Vanadinite is a powerful energizing crystal, known to enhance creativity, energy and vitality. It promotes great inner strength and stability, bringing a sense of support and security during times of stress. Vanadinite is also known to attract happiness, abundance and success to one's life.

HEALING PROPERTIES

- Energy
- Creativity
- Vitality
- Strength
- Passion

COLOUR AND FORMATION

Vanadinite forms as small hexagonal crystals growing in clusters on a matrix (a finer grained material in which larger crystals are embedded). Vanadinite crystals may be translucent or opaque, and often display brilliant shades of red and orange.

SOURCE AND HISTORY

First discovered in the 1800s, vanadinite is found in the United States, Mexico, Morocco and South Africa. It has become a favourite among collectors and healers, due to its brilliant colour and structure, as well as its powerful healing properties.

USE FOR

Vanadinite is an excellent stone to use during meditation. It carries a soothing and grounding energy that will facilitate deep inner peace, thereby allowing you to remain centred and focused.

HOME AND SPACE

Kept in the office or workspace, vanadinite helps with organization, physical energy and mental clarity. It also enhances levels of creativity and motivation, while keeping your mind free of distraction.

CHAKRA AND BODY

Vanadinite is a powerful stone for the root and sacral chakras. Its grounding energy brings a sense of comfort and balance while promoting vitality, confidence and self-expression.

LEFT vanadinite

RIGHT garnet

TRY THIS Wear vanadinite to promote confidence, stability and inner strength. Place garnet in a crystal grid (see page 174) to detoxify and purify the space of negative energy.

Garnet For Courage

Garnet is a powerful energizing and purifying stone, known to bring emotional balance, strength and vitality while also enhancing creativity and passion. Garnet is also a stone of protection, bringing a strong sense of security and stability.

HEALING PROPERTIES
- Energy
- Strength
- Courage
- Vitality
- Protection

COLOUR AND FORMATION
Garnet is recognized primarily for its beautiful red colour. However, it may also form in other tones of yellow, brown, orange, green and pink. These crystals are often small and may appear transparent, translucent or opaque.

SOURCE AND HISTORY
Garnet can be found worldwide, however, it is most commonly found in Canada, the United States, Brazil, Madagascar, South Africa, Sri Lanka and India. Garnet has a strong connection to many cultures throughout history: for the Egyptians, Greeks and Romans, it was considered to be a warrior's stone and was worn as a talisman of protection, courage and strength.

USE FOR
Wearing this stone is a powerful way to experience its many healing properties. It is known as a stone of commitment, promoting strong and lasting relationships. Wear or carry garnet to encourage independence and self-confidence while also strengthening the love and connection between two people.

HOME AND SPACE
Garnet is a stone of abundance and will attract success to a career or business. Keep this stone in the office or workspace to boost energy levels and creativity, as well as motivation and inspiration.

CHAKRA AND BODY
Garnet works primarily with the root chakra, bringing balance and stability as well as passion, creativity and energy.

TRY THIS Place tiger's eye in a crystal grid (see page 174) to attract positive energy and warmth into a space.

WORKS WELL WITH Tiger's eye and citrine (see page 55) make a powerful combination for fostering abundance and good fortune.

Tiger's Eye For Self-Confidence

Believed to carry the energies of the Earth and the sun, tiger's eye is a powerful stone. It is grounding and protecting and encourages self-confidence, courage and willpower. Tiger's eye is a strong amplifier of energy, increasing vitality and motivation.

HEALING PROPERTIES
- Protection
- Confidence
- Courage
- Manifestation
- Abundance

COLOUR AND FORMATION
Tiger's eye contains an iridescent golden hue, often with bands of yellow or brown that tend to resemble a cat's eye.

SOURCE AND HISTORY
This stone is found in the United States, Mexico, Brazil, South Africa, India and Australia. A popular stone throughout many cultures, tiger's eye was considered to be a stone of good luck and protection and was carried in battle by the ancient Romans as a symbol of bravery.

USE FOR
Wearing tiger's eye is an effective way of utilizing its energy. Having this stone close to you will increase your energy levels and will promote inner strength when going through times of stress. Tiger's eye is also a powerful manifestation stone and will amplify your intentions.

HOME AND SPACE
Keep this stone in the office or workspace, as it is known to attract abundance and good fortune. It also enhances mental clarity and increases the willpower to succeed.

CHAKRA AND BODY
Tiger's eye works strongly with the sacral chakra, enhancing the flow of passion and creativity.

Carnelian For Stability & Strength

Carnelian carries a powerful energy of stability and strength. It is known to increase vitality, courage and creativity while bringing a deep sense of warmth, happiness and wellbeing.

HEALING PROPERTIES
- Strength
- Courage
- Stability
- Passion
- Creativity

USE FOR
Wear carnelian to instil confidence, courage and stability. It is a high-energy stone that will eliminate emotional fatigue while encouraging you to feel more inspired and energetic throughout the day.

COLOUR AND FORMATION
This is a beautiful vibrant and translucent stone, which is formed in rough masses, often with a vitreous lustre. Its colour may vary between tones of orange, peach and red.

HOME AND SPACE
Carnelian increases energy levels and motivation, making it a useful stone to keep in the office or workspace. This stone will enhance passion and creativity, at the same time attracting abundance and wealth.

SOURCE AND HISTORY
Carnelian is found in the United States, Peru, Brazil, Great Britain, South Africa, Madagascar and India. A revered stone of power and protection, carnelian was placed in ancient Egyptian tombs to ensure a safe passage into the afterlife.

CHAKRA AND BODY
Carnelian activates the root chakra, increasing vitality, creativity and passion. This stone is known to balance hormones and increase fertility.

Kyanite For Self-Expression

A powerful amplifier of energy, kyanite carries a high spiritual vibration that encourages self-expression and open communication. This stone also has a calming effect on the mind and emotions, while creating an even flow of energy throughout the body.

HEALING PROPERTIES

- Communication
- Manifestation
- Intuition
- Tranquility
- Truth

COLOUR AND FORMATION

Blue kyanite is the most common variety of this stone; however, it can also occur in black, orange, green and pink. It appears as raw, bladed crystals that may be opaque or transparent, often with a pearlescent sheen.

SOURCE AND HISTORY

Kyanite is commonly found in the United States, Mexico, Brazil, Italy and Australia. Valued for its resistance to heat, kyanite is often used to create jewellery and other decorative objects.

USE FOR

Use this wonderful stone to facilitate meditation, as it creates a calm and tranquil space. This can be especially helpful to those who are learning to meditate. It will also assist you in developing psychic abilities and will enhance your intuition while keeping you calm, centred and focused.

HOME AND SPACE

Keep kyanite in the bedroom to promote peaceful sleep. This stone eliminates stress and physical fatigue, and so will enable you to wake up feeling rested and refreshed.

CHAKRA AND BODY

Kyanite will bring all seven chakras into alignment, keeping your body, mind and emotions feeling balanced.

Aquamarine For Soothing

Aquamarine carries the soothing and cleansing powers of the sea. It has a gentle calming energy that reduces stress and anxiety while enhancing inner strength and confidence. Aquamarine is also known for its anti-ageing properties and is often used in rejuvenating beauty rituals.

HEALING PROPERTIES

- Peace
- Rejuvenation
- Intuition
- Protection
- Abundance

COLOUR AND FORMATION

Aquamarine is a variety of beryl – a stone consisting of beryllium, aluminum and silicate. It forms as beautiful clear, hexagonal crystals that are light blue-green in colour.

SOURCE AND HISTORY

This crystal grows most abundantly in Brazil, South Africa, Madagascar and Russia. In ancient times, it was believed to be a stone of mermaids. Roman sailors would carry aquamarine as a talisman of protection against the sea and as a symbol of everlasting youth.

USE FOR

Due to its strong connection to water, aquamarine is a beautiful stone to use for cleansing. Whether used as an essence or during meditation, aquamarine allows you to reconnect with your true self, bringing a sense of inner peace.

HOME AND SPACE

Placing aquamarine in a bedroom will create a calming and restful space. Keep a small piece under your pillow to help with insomnia.

CHAKRA AND BODY

Aquamarine activates the throat chakra. When placed over this area, it will help you to learn how to communicate positively, without anger or judgement.

TRY THIS Use amethyst in a healing essence (see page 172) to calm nervous energy.

WORKS WELL WITH Together, amethyst and celestite (see page 124) offer a powerful combination for reducing stress.

Amethyst For Calming the Mind

Amethyst has been much admired throughout history. With its powerful healing and cleansing abilities, it is one of the most popular stones used in crystal healing today. It is particularly known for calming the mind and has been used for centuries to provide relief from mental-health conditions, such as anxiety and depression.

HEALING PROPERTIES

- Peace
- Healing
- Balance
- Intuition
- Protection

COLOUR AND FORMATION

This crystal is a type of quartz and grows as transparent terminated crystals that form naturally in clusters, geodes or single points. It has a striking purple colour that can range from light lavender to deep violet.

SOURCE AND HISTORY

Amethyst is found in many places, including Canada, the United States, Brazil, Mexico, Europe, Zambia, Namibia and India. This crystal has been cherished over thousands of years for its beauty and powerful healing abilities. In ancient Egypt, amethyst was worn as a symbol of luxury and as protective charms against evil spirits, while ancient Greeks drank wine from goblets adorned in amethyst, as it was believed to prevent drunkenness.

USE FOR

With its high spiritual vibration, amethyst is the perfect stone to use during meditation to enhance spiritual awareness and promote a calm state of mind.

HOME AND SPACE

Many people find it helpful to keep amethyst in the bedroom to help counter anxiety-related insomnia. It is also effective for children who are afraid of the dark or have nightmares.

CHAKRA AND BODY

Amethyst activates the third eye and crown chakras. When placed on the forehead, it will help to enhance your intuition and provide an overall sense of balance and mental clarity.

TRY THIS Wear celestite in a necklace to protect against anxiety and emotional imbalance.

WORKS WELL WITH Celestite and amethyst (see page 122) combine well to protect against anxiety and depression.

Celestite For Spiritual Awareness

Celestite carries a beautiful calming energy that teaches patience and promotes spiritual awareness. It encourages open communication and self-expression, allowing the development of inner strength and confidence. Celestite also enhances mental clarity and emotional stability, making it an excellent stone to protect against anxiety and depression.

HEALING PROPERTIES

- Spirituality
- Communication
- Clarity
- Peace
- Harmony

COLOUR AND FORMATION

A very delicate stone with beautiful transparent crystals, celestite often forms in geodes or clusters. It is best-known for its sky-blue colour, however, it can also be found in red, white or yellow hues.

SOURCE AND HISTORY

Celestite can be found in Peru, Great Britain, Poland, Egypt and Madagascar. The name celestite derives from the Latin word *caelestis* meaning 'celestial' or 'heavenly'. Traditionally the stone was used as a way to communicate with angelic realms.

USE FOR

This is a wonderful stone to use during meditation. It is an effective anti-anxiety tool and will allow you to replace any negative feelings with inner peace.

HOME AND SPACE

Keep celestite in the bedroom to create a tranquil and harmonious place of rest. If you have trouble sleeping, hold celestite for a moment before you go to sleep to release any stress from the day.

CHAKRA AND BODY

Celestite is a wonderful stone to balance the crown, third eye and throat chakras, promoting mental clarity and emotional balance.

Howlite For Peace and Stability

Howlite carries a beautiful calming energy that is especially helpful in reducing anxiety, tension and stress. It is a stone of peace and stability, teaching the importance of patience and promoting a higher state of spiritual and emotional awareness.

HEALING PROPERTIES

- Tranquility
- Peace
- Patience
- Stability
- Mindfulness

COLOUR AND FORMATION

Howlite usually forms as an opaque white or grey stone. It is often webbed with darker grey or brown, creating a beautiful marble effect.

SOURCE AND HISTORY

Howlite was first discovered in 1868 by Henry How, a Canadian chemist and mineralogist, for whom the stone was named after. This mineral is found in Canada, the United States, Mexico, Germany and Russia. Howlite has since become a popular stone for its many healing properties.

USE FOR

This is a powerful stone to use during meditation, as it calms the mind and encourages a deep meditative state. It is a very relaxing stone that will expand your consciousness while encouraging the release of any unhealthy attachments, negative energy or self-doubt.

HOME AND SPACE

This stone is particularly helpful for those who have trouble quietening their minds before going to bed. Keep the stone in the bedroom or under your pillow for a deep and restful sleep.

CHAKRA AND BODY

Howlite activates the crown and third eye chakras, heightening intuition and spiritual awareness while increasing mental clarity and focus.

> **TRY THIS** Use howlite in an essence (see page 172) before going to bed as a cure for insomnia. Place black tourmaline near your front door to protect against negative energy entering your home.

Black Tourmaline For Grounding and Protection

Also known as schorl, black tourmaline, is one of the most powerful
stones for protection. It carries a grounding energy that brings a deep
sense of balance and stability. This crystal also cleanses the mind of
negative thought patterns and eliminates stress, tension and anxiety.

HEALING PROPERTIES

- Protection
- Stability
- Balance
- Courage
- Strength

COLOUR AND FORMATION

Black tourmaline is a dense, opaque stone,
often with a shiny surface. It may also
contain vertical striations – narrow grooves
or ridges that are formed due to the stones'
growth pattern – which is common in all
types of tourmaline. These variations may
be transparent with a variety of colours
including blue, green, red, yellow and pink.

SOURCE AND HISTORY

This crystal can be found in the United
States, Brazil, South Africa, Pakistan,
Sri Lanka and Australia. It has been used
since the Middle Ages and has long been
recognized as a powerful talisman of
protection by Native American and African
tribes. In ancient Rome, black tourmaline
was also used for its calming properties,
encouraging restful sleep and relaxation.

USE FOR

Black tourmaline is a popular stone for
use during meditation. It is exceptionally
grounding and will help clear the mind of
any unwanted distraction. With its strong
cleansing abilities, this crystal also dissolves
negative energy from its environment,
creating a tranquil space of peace and
healing.

HOME AND SPACE

Keep this crystal in the office or workspace,
especially if you work on a computer, as it
protects against electromagnetic radiation. It
also increases energy levels and motivation
while attracting good luck and abundance.

CHAKRA AND BODY

Black tourmaline is strongly connected to
the root chakra, allowing you to feel secure
and grounded while increasing strength and
vitality.

BLACK STONES black tourmaline

WHITE/GREY STONES howlite

TRY THIS Meditate with lepidolite to encourage emotional healing and stability.

WORKS WELL WITH Pair lepidolite with smoky quartz (see page 136) to clear negative energy from your environment and to increase feelings of openness and contentment.

Lepidolite For Lightheartedness

Lepidolite is a true calming stone that is widely known for its ability to eliminate feelings of anxiety and depression. Its soothing energy attracts happiness and lightheartedness while promoting a positive mindset of gratitude and abundance.

HEALING PROPERTIES

- Peace
- Tranquility
- Healing
- Balance
- Happiness

COLOUR AND FORMATION

A form of mica, lepidolite is recognized by its beautiful pink or lilac hue. It often forms in translucent layered flakes, emitting a beautiful pearlescent glow.

SOURCE AND HISTORY

First discovered in the eighteenth century, lepidolite is found in the United States, the Dominican Republic, Brazil, Greenland and Madagascar. It is an important source of lithium, a metal that is used in a variety of mood-stabilizing medications today.

USE FOR

This is a powerful stone to wear or carry with you, especially during times of grief or loss. Wearing lepidolite will help alleviate emotional pain naturally, and is a wonderful way to utilize the strong healing energy of this mineral.

HOME AND SPACE

Since lepidolite is known primarily for its calming abilities, it a useful stone to keep in the bedroom. Its light and tranquil energy will bring peace and harmony into the space. Keeping it beside your bed will allow you to wake up feeling refreshed and positive.

CHAKRA AND BODY

Lepidolite activates the crown and third eye chakras. It will strengthen your intuition and increase mental clarity.

TRY THIS Wear or carry scolecite to eliminate feelings of stress, tension or anxiety.

WORKS WELL WITH Pair scolecite with apophyllite (see page 88) to enhance mental clarity and spiritual awareness.

Scolecite For Serenity

Scolecite carries a high spiritual vibration that facilitates personal growth and healing. It is a powerful stone for the mind and emotions, bringing a deep sense of peace and serenity that will eliminate feelings of stress and anxiety.

HEALING PROPERTIES

- Peace
- Healing
- Transformation
- Serenity
- Harmony

COLOUR AND FORMATION

This beautiful translucent crystal forms naturally in delicate needle-like sprays. It is often white, but may also occur in light shades of pink, red, green and yellow.

SOURCE AND HISTORY

First discovered in 1813, scolecite is found in Brazil, Iceland, Spain, South Africa, India and Russia. It is popular due to its beautiful healing properties and striking appearance.

USE FOR

Scolecite is a powerful stone to use during meditation. It brings peace and stillness, clearing your mind of any distraction, while encouraging a deeper state of meditation.

HOME AND SPACE

Keep this stone in the bedroom: placing a small piece under your pillow will calm the mind and allow you to fall asleep easily.

CHAKRA AND BODY

Scolecite is a crystal for the third eye and crown chakras. It will assist in strengthening your intuition while promoting a higher level of consciousness.

Chlorite For Cleansing Spaces

Chlorite is a powerful healing and cleansing stone. It removes negativity of all kinds, creating a positive and energized space. This crystal brings balance to the emotions and eliminates unwanted feelings of anger, jealousy, resentment or frustration.

HEALING PROPERTIES

- Healing
- Purity
- Positivity
- Protection
- Balance

COLOUR AND FORMATION

Chlorite is a forest-green mineral that can form inside quartz crystals, displaying unique phantoms or cloud-like inclusions.

SOURCE AND HISTORY

This stone can be found in the United States, Brazil, Germany, Madagascar and Russia. The stone is a favourite among many due to its powerful healing abilities, along with its strong connection to nature. Historically, it was believed by the Celtic druids that the energy of chlorite would promote a deeper connection to plants and animals as well as fairies, nymphs and other nature spirits.

USE FOR

Place chlorite crystals in a crystal grid (see page 174) to keep a space free of chaotic or stagnant energy. The stone will encourage a deep sense of peace and tranquility within its environment.

HOME AND SPACE

Keep chlorite in any room that you wish to cleanse and purify. It is a powerful detoxifying crystal and will create a powerful environment for physical and emotional healing.

CHAKRA AND BODY

Chlorite is a wonderful stone to align all seven chakras. The stone will clear energy blockages, bringing each chakra into alignment.

Selenite For Inner Peace

Carrying a calming and purifying energy, selenite cleanses the mind of any negativity and brings a deep sense of inner peace. It is known as a powerful stone of luck and protection, absorbing any negative energy while emanating light and peaceful vibrations.

HEALING PROPERTIES

- Peace
- Positivity
- Luck
- Protection
- Intuition

COLOUR AND FORMATION

Selenite is a variety of gypsum, a soft sulfate mineral, that is often translucent with a reflective shimmer. Its colours can range from pure white to earthy tones of orange, brown or green.

SOURCE AND HISTORY

This crystal is found in the United States, Mexico, England, Germany, Poland, Greece, Russia and Australia. Throughout history, this shimmering stone has long been associated with the moon. In ancient Greece, selenite was believed to be the stone of the moon goddess, Selene, from which it takes it name.

USE FOR

Bringing clarity to the mind and emotions, selenite is a powerful stone to use during meditation. A stone of spiritual transformation, it will encourage a deeper sense of spiritual understanding.

HOME AND SPACE

Placing a selenite crystal in each corner of the home is a wonderful way to utilize its protective qualities. Used in this way, this cleansing crystal will clear the space of negative energy while attracting light and positivity into the atmosphere.

CHAKRA AND BODY

Selenite is a crystal primarily associated with the crown chakra, expanding consciousness and heightening intuition.

IN FRONT chlorite
BEHIND selenite

TRY THIS Place a piece of labradorite under your pillow to increase psychic abilities or other intuitive gifts.

WORKS WELL WITH Labradorite and moonstone (see page 150) are considered sister stones and combine wonderfully to facilitate emotional balance and healing.

Labradorite For Protection

Labradorite is a powerful stone of protection and personal transformation. It guards against negative energy of all kinds and eliminates bad habits or thought patterns, allowing you to develop and transform both emotionally and spiritually.

HEALING PROPERTIES

- Protection
- Transformation
- Spirituality
- Strength
- Intuition

COLOUR AND FORMATION

Labradorite most often appears as a dark, opaque stone with bright iridescent flashes of green, blue or gold. Another variety of this crystal, spectrolite, displays a full spectrum of colours including pink, purple, red and yellow.

SOURCE AND HISTORY

This crystal can be found in Canada, the United States, Greenland, Finland, Italy, Russia and Madagascar. Labradorite was believed by various cultures to be a stone of magic, including the native Inuit tribes of North America who used it to cure illness.

USE FOR

Wearing labradorite is the most effective way of benefitting from its many healing properties. The stone encourages spiritual expansion and increases your intuitive abilities. It promotes personal growth and inner strength while allowing you to remain grounded and focused.

HOME AND SPACE

Labradorite is particularly beneficial for your professional life. In the workplace it brings energy, creativity and inspiration, encouraging a productive and enthusiastic environment. The crystal also promotes a sense of adventure and imagination when working on new ideas and projects.

CHAKRA AND BODY

This crystal activates the crown, third eye and throat chakras, encouraging spiritual transformation, mental clarity and positive communication.

TRY THIS Place smoky quartz in a crystal grid (see page 174) to protect against negative energy entering your home.

WORKS WELL WITH Pair smoky quartz with amethyst (see page 122) to ease emotional stress and to bring balance into your life.

Smoky Quartz For Detoxification

Smoky quartz is one of the most powerful stones of protection. It is a strong detoxifier and removes negative or toxic energy from its surroundings. Smoky quartz also carries a healing and grounding vibration, bringing a sense of balance and stability during times of stress.

HEALING PROPERTIES
- Protection
- Healing
- Stability
- Growth
- Vitality

COLOUR AND FORMATION
Smoky quartz holds a similar translucence to other types of quartz. Crystals can be found in points or clusters of any size and are recognized by their soothing earthy hues of grey or brown.

SOURCE AND HISTORY
Found in most parts of the world, including the United States, Mexico, Brazil, South Africa, Madagascar and Australia, smoky quartz has featured in many different cultures over hundreds of years. The crystal was regarded as a symbol of the Earth gods and goddesses by the ancient druids and has a long history of being used as a talisman of protection.

USE FOR
Wear or carry smoky quartz when you need a sense of stability in your life. This stone is known for its strong ability to filter out negative energy of all kinds and will help to reduce feelings of anxiety, depression, fear or jealousy.

HOME AND SPACE
This is a wonderful crystal to keep in the office or workspace. Mentally, it will enhance focus and concentration, while helping to sustain your energy levels throughout the day. If you work around computers, smoky quartz will also protect against electromagnetic pollution.

CHAKRA AND BODY
Smoky quartz activates the root chakra, promoting emotional balance and calmness. This crystal will also increase creativity, vitality and passion throughout many areas of your life.

Turquoise For Protection

Quite possibly the oldest and most sacred of all stones, turquoise is primarily used as a talisman of purification and protection due to its powerful energy to guard against negative forces. It has a strong healing vibration that instils an inner calm, bringing emotional stability and relief from anxiety.

HEALING PROPERTIES
- Protection
- Balance
- Tranquility
- Creativity
- Communication

COLOUR AND FORMATION
Turquoise forms as an opaque stone with a vibrant blue-green colour, often containing natural brown or cream webbing.

SOURCE AND HISTORY
This crystal is found primarily in the United States, Mexico, Egypt, Iran, Afghanistan and China. It has been regarded as a protective stone for thousands of years, and was worn as a symbol of royalty, honour and wisdom by the rulers of ancient Egypt, including Cleopatra. Other cultures and civilizations – including the Aztecs and Native Americans – have worn turquoise as a talisman of luck, power and success.

USE FOR
Turquoise is a useful stone to carry when travelling, as it protects against accidents and mishaps. It also promotes clear thinking and provides relief from anxiety if you are fearful of flying.

HOME AND SPACE
Keep turquoise in the office or workspace to encourage clear communication, self-expression and creativity. This is especially helpful when you are feeling creatively blocked or are in need of inspiration.

CHAKRA AND BODY
Turquoise balances and aligns all seven chakras. However, since it is a stone of communication, wisdom and truth, it is particularly helpful when activating the throat chakra.

TRY THIS Wear turquoise in a necklace to feel confident, energized and balanced throughout your day.
Wear larimar in a necklace to encourage personal growth, forgiveness and clear communication.

Larimar For Tranquility

A soft and peaceful stone, larimar brings a deep sense of tranquility. It carries a beautiful healing energy that calms the mind and eliminates feelings of stress and anxiety. Larimar's ethereal vibration also raises consciousness and promotes a deeper connection to nature.

HEALING PROPERTIES
- Tranquility
- Peace
- Wisdom
- Rejuvenation
- Stability

COLOUR AND FORMATION
Larimar is a translucent blue-green stone that is often webbed with white to create beautiful water-like patterns. It is formed deep in volcanic tubes, however due to soil erosion and rainfall, stones can also be found in the sea.

SOURCE AND HISTORY
Found only in the Dominican Republic, larimar was first discovered in 1916 by Miguel Mendez and Norman Riling. Mendez named the stone 'larimar', combining his daughter's name, Larissa, and *mar*, the Spanish word for sea. Before this official discovery, the locals and their ancestors had long been aware of the stone. It was first said that larimar came from the sea, and later that it came from the Earth's volcanic movements.

USE FOR
This is a beautiful stone to use during meditation, prompting the mind to drift into a deeper meditative state. It is a powerful stone to assist in emotional healing and encourages the release of negative attachments, people or habits that are no longer of benefit to you.

HOME AND SPACE
Since larimar is a calming stone, it is best kept in the bedroom. Placing a small piece under your pillow will promote restful sleep, allowing you to wake up feeling refreshed and rejuvenated.

CHAKRA AND BODY
This is a powerful stone for the higher chakras, particularly the throat and heart, where it will stimulate open communication and self-expression while healing and releasing emotional pain.

Aragonite For Stability

A grounding stone, aragonite brings a sense of comfort and stability.
It carries a calming energy that provides great strength and support
during times of stress. This crystal also holds a deep connection to the
Earth and is a helpful stone for restoring emotional balance and harmony.

HEALING PROPERTIES

- Strength
- Stability
- Balance
- Harmony
- Growth

COLOUR AND FORMATION

Aragonite appears in multiple forms, often in
translucent star-like clusters. Its colour can
also vary, ranging in earthy tones of white,
yellow, orange, blue, pink or green.

SOURCE AND HISTORY

Aragonite was named after the Aragon River
in Spain, where it was first discovered in
1788. Sources of this crystal can be found in
Mexico, Spain, Great Britain and Namibia.

USE FOR

Aragonite is a powerful stone to use
during meditation for personal growth. Its
grounding and balancing energy attracts
warmth and brightness, eliminating negative
feelings of fear, anger or resentment.
It is also a stone of spiritual expansion,
sharpening intuition and bringing a state of
peace and harmony.

HOME AND SPACE

Keep aragonite in the workspace, where
it will inspire creativity, passion and focus.
It will also encourage a higher level of
commitment and responsibility. Known as a
useful stone for artists of all kinds, aragonite
will bring inspiration at times when drive or
enthusiasm is lacking.

CHAKRA AND BODY

Aragonite resonates primarily with the
sacral and root chakras, bringing balance
and stability, but also passion and creativity.

LARGER STONES obsidian
STAR CLUSTERS aragonite

TRY THIS Sleep with aragonite under your pillow to help with insomnia. Use obsidian in an essence (see page 172) to improve focus and increase energy flow.

Obsidian For Strength and Protection

A strong stone of protection and strength, obsidian creates a shield against negativity of all kinds while cleansing and purifying the energy within its environment. Obsidian carries a grounding vibration, assisting in emotional healing and encouraging personal growth.

HEALING PROPERTIES

- Protection
- Energy
- Balance
- Strength
- Growth

COLOUR AND FORMATION

This shiny opaque stone forms from volcanic lava that has quickly cooled. It can be found in a range of earthy tones, including black, brown, green or mahogany.

SOURCE AND HISTORY

Obsidian is found in many different locations around the world, including the United States, Mexico, Scotland, Greece, Kenya, Japan, Papua New Guinea, Australia and New Zealand. It has been used by many cultures since prehistoric times for making arrowheads, knives, spear points and other cutting tools due its durability and naturally sharp edges. The Aztecs not only used obsidian for weaponry, but also believed in the healing powers of the stone. They would use a balm that contained powdered obsidian to heal scars.

USE FOR

Wearing obsidian helps to draw out anxiety or stress, replacing any scattered energy with a sense of peace and harmony. Obsidian also removes tension from a relationship and will eliminate negative feelings of jealousy, anger or bitterness.

HOME AND SPACE

Placing a piece of obsidian above the front door will help protect against negative energy entering the home.

CHAKRA AND BODY

Obsidian is primarily associated with the root chakra and allows you to feel centred, balanced and grounded within yourself.

Fire Agate For Support and Security

Fire agate carries a strengthening and stabilizing energy that encourages a deep sense of inner balance. It is also a strong grounding and protecting stone that provides support and security during difficult times.

HEALING PROPERTIES

- Strength
- Stability
- Protection
- Support
- Passion

COLOUR AND FORMATION

This is a beautiful translucent stone with red, orange and brown hues. It often contains swirling, flame-like patterns, as well as iridescent flashes of gold, red and yellow.

SOURCE AND HISTORY

Fire agate is found in the United States, Mexico, Brazil, Iceland, Morocco and India. Historically, this stone was believed to carry the essence of fire and was often used in Egyptian alchemy, the ancient practice attempting to transmute ordinary metals into gold.

USE FOR

Wear fire agate to instil courage, confidence and stability. This stone will create a protective shield against any negative energy and its soothing vibration will allow you to feel safe and secure in all aspects of your life.

HOME AND SPACE

Keep this stone in the bedroom to encourage passion in a relationship and to increase vitality. It is a helpful support stone and will assist in eliminating any fear or anxiety related to emotional or physical intimacy.

CHAKRA AND BODY

Fire agate activates the root and sacral chakras, increasing physical energy, vitality, passion and confidence.

TRY THIS Use fire agate in an essence (see page 172) to promote emotional strength, energy and courage.

WORKS WELL WITH Combined with carnelian (see page 116) fire agate promotes sexuality, self-confidence and creativity.

Onyx For Strength and Stability

Onyx is a grounding stone that brings strength and stability. It carries a strong energy of protection, guarding against negativity of all kinds. Onyx also builds self-confidence and enhances vitality.

HEALING PROPERTIES

- Protection
- Strength
- Stability
- Vitality
- Confidence

COLOUR AND FORMATION

Although onyx is usually black, it is also found in earthy tones of brown, grey, white or red. It is an opaque stone, often with lighter bands or stripes.

SOURCE AND HISTORY

Sources of onyx exist in the United States, Mexico, Brazil, South Africa, Madagascar and India. It is an ancient stone that has been used for thousands of years as a symbol of protection. The ancient Romans carried amulets of onyx into battle as a symbol of courage.

USE FOR

Wear or carry onyx to create a protective shield against negativity: wearing onyx will allow you to remain grounded and free of stress. Draw on its power to enhance strength and energy when feeling lethargic or unwell.

HOME AND SPACE

Keep onyx in any room of the home to purify and balance the energy within the space. This stone will promote spiritual and emotional transformation, encouraging deep reflection and self-improvement.

CHAKRA AND BODY

Onyx is closely associated with the root chakra, bringing stability, strength and vitality.

TRY THIS Keep onyx by your bed to prevent nightmares or insomnia. This crystal is useful for children who are afraid of the dark.

WORKS WELL WITH Onyx and sugilite (see page 80) make a powerful combination for raising strength and support during times of grief or loss.

TRY THIS Use sapphire in an essence
(see page 172) to cleanse the body of
toxins and impurities.

WORKS WELL WITH Pair sapphire with
ruby (see page 73) to promote faithfulness,
love and loyalty in a relationship.

Sapphire For Protection from Harm

Considered a sacred stone in Buddhism, sapphire symbolizes wisdom, royalty, honour and truth. It carries an energy of peace and purity, encouraging mental clarity and peace of mind. Known as a stone of protection, sapphire also eliminates negative energy and releases unwanted tension and stress.

HEALING PROPERTIES

- Protection
- Strength
- Wisdom
- Peace
- Purity

COLOUR AND FORMATION

This crystal is best-known for its beautiful vibrant blue. However, variations include green, black, yellow, pink and violet stones. Sapphire can appear completely transparent, or cloudy and opaque.

SOURCE AND HISTORY

Sapphire can be found in Brazil, Madagascar, India, Sri Lanka and Australia. It is one of the most prized stones in history and has been referenced in almost every culture and religion for centuries. The crystal was traditionally worn by royal families of ancient Rome and Greece for protection against harm of all kinds, including poison, witchcraft and evil spirits.

USE FOR

Wear sapphire to attract positivity and abundance. The stone will enhance your intuition while increasing memory, focus and intellect. Sapphire is also an effective purifying stone, cleansing the mind and emotions from negative energy of all kinds.

HOME AND SPACE

Sapphire is an effective stone to keep in the office or workspace, as it promotes a positive flow of balanced energy. It is also believed to attract abundance and prosperity while increasing creativity and mental acuity.

CHAKRA AND BODY

Primarily associated with the third eye and throat chakras, sapphire facilitates self-expression and open communication.

Hematite For Harmony

Hematite is a stone of protection and balance. It carries a grounding energy that brings harmony to the mind, body and emotions. This crystal also enhances willpower and courage, especially for those who lack confidence in themselves.

HEALING PROPERTIES
- Protection
- Courage
- Stability
- Support
- Confidence

COLOUR AND FORMATION
An opaque mineral, hematite may be red or silver with a metallic sheen. It may also form in quartz crystals, creating beautiful phantoms or inclusions.

SOURCE AND HISTORY
Hematite is found in Canada, the United States, Brazil, Great Britain, Sweden, Switzerland, Italy and Australia. It has a long history of various uses throughout many cultures. In ancient Egypt, the crystal was powdered and used as paint to decorate the tombs of pharaohs, while the early Romans would rub crushed hematite over their bodies, believing that it would bestow courage, strength and protection.

USE FOR
Use hematite during meditation to remain emotionally and spiritually centred. The stone will eliminate feelings of stress and anxiety, allowing you to feel a deeper sense of peace and stability.

HOME AND SPACE
Place a hematite crystal in each corner of the home to prevent negative energy from entering your space.

CHAKRA AND BODY
Hematite is primarily associated with the root chakra, stabilizing the mind and emotions while encouraging a greater connection to the Earth.

TRY THIS Wear hematite to remain grounded and centred. This stone will also increase confidence and self-esteem.

WORKS WELL WITH Hematite and black tourmaline (see page 127) make an extremely powerful combination for protecting against negative energy of all kinds.

TRY THIS Use moonstone in a crystal grid (see page 174) to attract new love or to bring harmony into a relationship that has become unstable.

WORKS WELL WITH Moonstone works beautifully with garnet (see page 113) to attract abundance and happiness.

Moonstone For Peace and Healing

Moonstone is considered a stone of protection, peace and healing. It carries a light and nurturing energy that calms the mind and brings comfort during times of stress. Moonstone also enhances intuition and will encourage spiritual and personal growth.

HEALING PROPERTIES
- Protection
- Peace
- Healing
- Intuition
- Harmony

COLOUR AND FORMATION
This crystal occurs in varying shades of white, grey, yellow, peach, blue, green or black. These beautiful stones are often translucent with iridescent flashes of silver and blue.

SOURCE AND HISTORY
Moonstone is found in many parts of the world, including Canada, Madagascar, India, Russia, Sri Lanka and Australia. It has been used for thousands of years as an amulet of good fortune and protection. The ancient Greeks used moonstone to represent the moon goddess, Selene.

USE FOR
Wearing moonstone is a wonderful way to feel its positive healing effects; as a crystal of protection, it can be carried during travel to protect against accidents. It is known to carry feminine energies, making it a powerful support crystal for women. Moonstone is also said to balance the hormones and bring harmony to the mind and emotions.

HOME AND SPACE
Keep moonstone in the bedroom to help with insomnia and to create a loving and relaxed environment.

CHAKRA AND BODY
Moonstone is primarily associated with the crown chakra. This stone allows you to develop emotional awareness and will heighten your intuition.

CHAPTER 3

USING YOUR CRYSTALS

An Introduction to Using Crystals

Every crystal is unique in colour, texture, shape and structure – all elements that play a role in creating the healing vibration of a particular stone. The vibrations connect us to the Earth, teaching us the power of intention and encouraging us to grow, transform and trust in our own intuition.

Each stone carries a unique energy that can be used for a specific healing purpose. Whether you are working with a protection stone, such as black tourmaline, or a crystal of abundance, such as citrine, incorporating a crystal into a simple ritual or daily routine is a powerful way to harness the healing properties of these beautiful objects. These rituals will encourage you to programme each crystal and set intentions for it: by dedicating a stone to a specific purpose, you will develop a greater connection to its energy while infusing it with pure intention.

From essences and beauty treatments to grids (placing stones in a symmetrical pattern to amplify a specific purpose or intention) and body layouts (laying stones on or around the body), crystals can be used in a variety of different ways to promote physical and emotional health and wellbeing. Use your intuition to discover which crystals resonate with your own energy and experiment with different ways of bringing them into your life. For example, an amethyst crystal is a calming stone that activates the third eye chakra when used during meditation; clear quartz acts as an energy amplifier that increases the healing vibration of other stones around it, making it a powerful crystal to use in grids or body layouts. Use this chapter to gain a unique insight to key rituals and healing methods that you can use to enhance your own crystal healing experience.

Meditation

Meditation is a simple yet powerful exercise that can have many benefits on our lives – from helping to manage stress to increasing energy and productivity. For centuries, meditation has been fundamental not only in gaining spiritual enlightenment, but also in maintaining physical health and emotional wellbeing. Practising meditation, even for just ten minutes a day, allows you to recharge and clear your mind.

Different meditation methods depend on personal preference. Some people like to repeat a mantra, while others choose to focus on their breathing or to concentrate on an intention or on the energy of the particular crystal they are using. Incorporating crystals into a meditation enables you to connect better with the stones, so deepening the whole meditative experience. Holding a clear quartz or amethyst crystal can bring clarity and focus while amplifying your intention (see page 28).

Crystals can also be used as a point of focus, allowing you to direct your energy and remain balanced and centred throughout your meditation.

When working with a specific intention or chakra, strengthen your meditation by incorporating a stone that resonates with that intention or activates the given chakra. For example, if you are meditating to encourage emotional healing, hold a rose quartz in each hand to open the heart chakra;. the crystal will then amplify the healing process. Experiment with a variety of crystals during meditation to see which ones feel right to you, as each carries its own healing vibration.

How to Meditate Using Crystals

Before sitting down to meditate, ensure your crystals are cleansed (see page 22) and programmed for whatever purpose you wish to achieve (see page 28).

WHAT YOU NEED

Cushion, mat or blanket
Crystal of choice

TIME

If you are new to meditation, try practising five to ten minutes a day initially. Once comfortable, increase to fifteen to twenty minutes a day, or for however long suits you.

METHOD

1   Find a quiet and comfortable place to sit and hold the crystals in your hands. Close your eyes and take a few deep breaths, allowing yourself to relax completely.

2   Once you are fully relaxed, bring your focus to the crystal you are holding, taking notice of its energy. Don't worry if your mind wanders, just gently bring your attention back whenever this happens.

3   As you breathe in and out, release any tension or stress you may be harbouring. Allow the energy of the crystal to flow throughout your body. You may feel the stone's energy resonating with a particular chakra.

4   When you are ready to open your eyes, take a few more deep breaths and experience a sense of calm and clarity before bringing awareness back to your surroundings.

Rituals

Whether part of a self-care routine or an ancient spiritual tradition, a ritual is a conscious action that is carried out for a specific purpose or outcome. Rituals promote consistency and mindfulness within our lives, while bringing a greater sense of motivation and commitment. They also encourage thoughtfulness as we go about our daily routines and this has a positive affect on our physical, emotional and spiritual wellbeing. Try one of the following rituals or devise one of your own.

New Moon Ritual

Aligning your intentions with the phases of the moon is a deeply powerful way to connect with youself and the universe. A new moon represents growth and renewal. It signifies a time for you to invite new energy into your life by setting goals and intentions for the month ahead. Incorporating healing crystals and other sacred objects into this ritual will amplify your intention and begin the manifestation process.

WHAT YOU NEED

Clear quartz crystal
Other sacred objects: a candle,
  incense, stones or flowers
Sage smudge stick or palo santo
  wood
Lighter or matches
Dish or abalone shell
Cushions or blankets
Pen and paper

TIME

This ritual should be performed on the night of a new moon. It is a simple practice and can be completed quite quickly, but you should allow up to one hour in order to feel fully relaxed and to have the time to incorporate as many elements as you like.

METHOD

1   Create a sacred space where there are no distractions, preferably outside. You may like to include incense, crystals and other objects that you feel connected to.

2   Cleanse the space using your sage smudge stick or palo santo wood (see page 162). Focus on clearing the energy around you before you begin the ritual. Use your dish to extinguish the flame gently.

3   Once you feel cleansed and relaxed, think about what you wish to achieve in the coming moon cycle and write it down on a piece of paper. This may be a list of goals or just one positive intention.

4   To complete the ritual, you may like to meditate on your intention(s) while holding the crystal. This will help you to begin the manifestation process.

5   Keep the piece of paper in your sacred space, or somewhere safe in the home, and return to it regularly so that you can read it for motivation.

TIP

Reading your list or intention out loud while holding a quartz crystal, will help you to begin the manifestation process.

Full Moon Ritual

The full moon brings a time of reflection. It encourages us to release what no longer serves us and makes way for bigger and brighter things to come. In recognizing what we need to let go of in our lives, we invite inner healing, cleansing and renewal. Incorporating healing crystals into a full moon ritual amplifies your intentions and facilitates the healing and transformation process.

WHAT YOU NEED

Clear quartz crystal
Other sacred objects: incense,
  stones or flowers
Sage smudge stick or palo santo
  wood
Lighter or matches
Dish or abalone shell
Cushions or blankets
Pen and paper
Candle

TIME

This ritual should be performed on the night of a full moon. It is a simple practice and can be completed quite quickly, but you should allow up to one hour in order to feel fully relaxed and to have the time to incorporate as many elements as you like.

METHOD

1   Create a sacred space where there are no distractions, preferably outside. You may like to include incense, crystals and other objects that you feel connected to.

2   Cleanse the space using your sage smudge stick or palo santo wood (see page 162). Focus on clearing the energy around you before you begin the ritual. Use your dish to extinguish the flame gently.

3   Once you feel cleansed and relaxed, reflect on the past two weeks since your new moon ritual and think about what you have achieved so far. Consider, also, anything that might be holding you back from achieving your goals.

4   Write down a list of what you want to release from your life. This may be a bad habit, negative thought patterns or even the name of a person that you need to let go of emotionally.

5   Using a candle, burn the piece of paper. As you do so, focus on releasing any negative energy from your life. Sit for a few moments and think about the ways in which releasing this negativity will benefit you in your life and allow you to move forward, refocusing on your intentions.

TIP

Cleanse and recharge your crystal
after performing this ritual (see
page 22), and leave it out under the
full moon until morning.

Space Clearing Ritual

This ritual is a wonderful way to cleanse your space of any stagnant or negative energy. By combining powerful cleansing tools such as sage, candles, selenite and black tourmaline, you can create a protective shield against negativity, while promoting balance, harmony and peace within your environment.

WHAT YOU NEED

4 black tourmaline stones, cleansed
4 selenite pieces, cleansed
Sage smudge stick
Lighter or matches
Dish or abalone shell

TIME

This ritual usually takes less than thirty minutes to complete, making it a quick and simple ritual to perform whenever you feel that your space is in need of some extra cleansing.

METHOD

1   Start by cleaning the space: declutter any drawers, sweep and clean any surfaces. Open all the windows and curtains, letting as much light and air in as possible. This step may feel underwhelming, however it is an important part of the ritual. You will feel the difference right away.

2   Take a moment to sit with your crystals, programming them so that they work powerfully together to clear the space.

3   Place one black tourmaline crystal and one selenite crystal in each corner of the space, creating an energetic shield against negativity. Black tourmaline is a powerful cleansing stone that will absorb unwanted energy, as well as electromagnetic fields. Selenite will amplify this process by helping to purify the space while emanating light and peaceful vibrations. Together they make a powerful space-clearing combination.

4   Light your sage smudge stick and cleanse yourself, moving the smoke in front, above and behind you (take extra care here). Now walk around the edge of the room, using the smoke to cleanse the entire space. Visualize the energy disintegrating and evaporating and use an affirmation like 'I only allow positive energy in my space'.

5   Use your dish to extinguish the sage smudge stick gently. Allow the crystals to sit for at least twelve hours before removing them and remember to cleanse each of them afterwards.

TIPS

If you have an altar or sacred space in your home, you may wish to light a candle or incense during this ritual as a way of amplifying your intention.

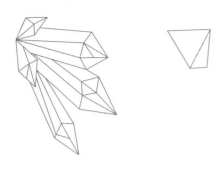

Chakras and Laying of Stones

Chakras are the energy centres of the body, working to provide an even energy that allows you to function at your best physically, emotionally and spiritually. When one of these energy centres is blocked, you can become unbalanced and disconnected. You can align your chakras through breath work and by practising yoga, as well as through crystal healing. Using crystals to align your chakras is a powerful way to bring balance and harmony to your mind and body.

Each crystal relates to a particular chakra depending on its colour and healing properties. Simply by placing a crystal over its corresponding chakra, you can effectively clear away any emotional or physical blockages. This technique is known as 'laying of stones', a ritual that has been practised for thousands of years.

By performing this technique each week, you can effectively clear away any emotional or physical imbalances. Start slowly, focusing on one chakra at a time for the first week, working from the base chakra up to the crown chakra. Once you are comfortable with this, you can then lay all seven stones at once, leaving them in place for at least fifteen minutes at a time. This can be a slower process for some people, while others might feel a change in energy flow almost immediately.

This chart explains the location of each chakra, what it means and some of its corresponding stones.

CHAKRA	LOCATION	COLOUR	RELATES TO	STONES
Root Chakra	Base of the spine	Red and black	Balance, stability, grounding, security, energy	Ruby, hematite, red jasper, garnet
Sacral Chakra	Below the navel	Orange	Sexuality, creativity, emotion, intuition	Carnelian, orange calcite, vanadinite
Solar Plexus Chakra	Upper abdomen	Yellow	Ambition, power, confidence, personality, intellect	Citrine, tiger's eye, pyrite
Heart Chakra	Centre of chest	Green and pink	Love, compassion, emotional balance	Chrysoprase, jade, rose quartz, rhodochrosite
Throat Chakra	Above the collarbone	Blue	Communication, expression, guidance	Sodalite, turquoise, aquamarine, blue calcite
Third Eye Chakra	Between the eyes	Indigo	Spiritual awareness, intuition, psychic power, focus	Amethyst, sugilite, lapis lazuli, blue sapphire
Crown Chakra	Top of the head	Lilac or white	Consciousness, enlightenment, unity, peace	Amethyst, lepidolite, clear quartz, diamond

Massages and Treatments

Crystals have been used as massage tools for centuries to promote balance and wellbeing, both physically and emotionally. By using the vibrations of various crystals during healing practices such as reflexology or gua sha, you can bring a deeper level of healing into your energy field, while also activating the function of cells, muscles and organs.

When using crystals in massage and other rituals, energy centres are also addressed, bringing balance to the chakras. Polished crystals such as spheres, wands and tumbled stones are most appropriate for this and can be incorporated into various massage techniques to promote energy flow throughout the entire body.

Reflexology-Inspired Massage

Reflexology is an ancient practice that involves massaging areas of the hands and feet as a way of communicating with a different part of the body. This massage technique is known to remove toxins, improve circulation and provide relief from stress. Incorporating crystals in reflexology is a way to enhance the treatment, targeting energy imbalances in the body, while also working to rebalance the chakras. Below is a simple crystal massage that can be practised on the hands or feet to improve energy flow throughout the body.

WHAT YOU NEED

Crystal-infused oil or essence of your choice

Rounded amethyst wand

TIME

Spend as much time as you like – up to twenty minutes is good. This is a wonderful relaxing exercise to try before bed or after your shower, when your muscles are more relaxed.

METHOD

1 Massage in your gem oil or essence, gently working over each section of your left hand.

2 Take your crystal wand and gently massage your hand using a circular clockwise motion, slowly relaxing the muscles while focusing on the healing energy of your stone.

3 Allow yourself to relax, feeling which areas hold more tension. Work these areas gently until you can apply more pressure.

4 Almost as if this was a form of meditation, take a few deep breaths and use this time to heal, reflect or release stress.

5 Repeat on your right hand.

TIP

This ritual uses an amethyst wand for its healing and calming properties. You may use whatever stone you feel most connected to for this purpose.

Gua Sha Facial Massage

Gua sha is an ancient Chinese healing practice that is used to increase blood flow, release toxins from the skin and reduce inflammation. It works by releasing tension in the muscles while breaking up any stagnant energy to promote healing and rejuvenation. To further enhance the healing benefits of this technique, the tools used in gua sha are often made from stones that contain anti-aging properties, such as rose quartz or jade. This powerful practice is a wonderful way to incorporate healing crystals into your beauty ritual for healthy, glowing skin.

WHAT YOU NEED

Rosehip oil, argan oil or a moisturizer

Rose quartz or jade gua sha facial massage tool

TIME

Allow yourself ten to fifteen minutes for this gua sha massage. You can practise this technique as often as you like, however two to three times a week will be plenty.

METHOD

1   Prepare your face by ensuring your skin is cleansed and free of any make-up or impurities.

2   Apply rosehip oil, argan oil or a moisturizer. This is an important step to make sure the massage tool glides over your skin easily without pulling.

3   Taking your massage tool, apply light pressure with the curved part and sweep evenly upwards from your eyebrows to the top of your hairline. Repeat each stroke three to five times, moving all the way along the hairline.

4   Now work beneath your eyes, on the left side of your face. Using the tool, start from the middle of your face, sweeping over the cheekbone and up to your temple. Always use an upward stroke, as you want to lift the skin. Repeat three to five times.

5   Still working on the left side of your face, use this same motion for the cheek area, starting from the inside of your nose, sweeping up to the ear. Repeat three to five times.

6   Repeat steps 4 and 5 on the right side of your face.

7   For the mouth and chin area, repeat this same sweeping motion, beginning from the centre of your face, up to your left, and then right, earlobe.

8   For your neck and under your chin, start under your jaw and work down to your collarbone.

TIP

You may also try this technique with a crystal massage wand or tumbled stone if you don't own a gua sha tool.

Crystals and Beauty

Crystals and gemstones can be used in a variety of ways to infuse your daily self-care routine with healing energy. Crystals help your cells thrive at an energetic level while giving your skin an extra healthy glow. Bring some amethyst or quartz crystals into the bath with you for an extra relaxing experience, or use aquamarine in a face mist to cleanse and brighten your complexion. Whichever way you wish to use them, the crystals' powerful vibrations will leave you feeling relaxed and restored.

Rose quartz and jade are two of the most powerful stones for cleansing and replenishing the skin. A jade or rose-quartz facial massage roller, for example, is known as an effective anti-aging tool that promotes healthy, glowing skin. It is believed that the ancient Egyptian Cleopatra bathed with rose quartz and often used it in facial masks to maintain her beauty.

Rose-Quartz-Infused Face Mask

Use this simple rose-quartz-infused facial mask to replenish and restore skin cells.

WHAT YOU NEED

1 or more raw rose quartz crystals
¼ glass of filtered or fresh water
Small bowl
2–3 drops rosehip oil
1 tsp of your favourite natural clay
    mask

TIME

Making this mask will take around twenty minutes. Once you have applied the mask, allow time for it to dry before washing it off.

METHOD

1 Start by preparing a simple crystal essence: add your crystals to the glass of water and leave in direct sunlight or moonlight for at least fifteen minutes.

2 Remove the crystals and transfer the water to a small bowl.

3 Add your rosehip oil and clay to the water and mix into a paste.

4 Apply evenly to your face, allowing it to dry before washing off.

TIP

Experiment with other crystals such as jade, amethyst or clear quartz.

CRYSTALS AND ANTI-AGEING

Certain crystals carry anti-ageing properties that can be incorporated into your skin care routine to replenish skin cells and prevent signs of ageing. There are a wide range of age-defying products available, such as facial rollers or gua sha tools made from jade, rose quartz or amethyst as well as crystal-infused moisturizers and cleansers. Other stones with anti-ageing effects include clear quartz, black tourmaline and aquamarine. You can use water infused with these gems in the bath or as a face wash, allowing the rejuvenating properties to absorb into the skin.

Crystal Essence

A crystal essence is a simple yet effective way of working with the healing energy of crystals and gemstones. When pure water is infused with crystal vibrations, it is then charged with the healing properties of the stone. This essence can be used to promote healing, wellness and to raise your own vibration. Try this simple recipe for a crystal essence that can be used with your choice of crystal to align with your own specific needs.

WHAT YOU NEED

1 or more crystals of your choice
Sage smudge stick or palo santo wood
Lighter or matches
¾ glass of fresh water
Jar
¼ glass of vodka
Small dropper bottle

TIME

Creating a crystal essence is a simple process that you can easily practise at home. Allow five to ten minutes for preparation and an extra hour or longer for infusion.

METHOD

1 Select the type of crystal you want to use for your essence based on its healing properties and what you need them for. Keep in mind that some stones can be toxic or may crumble in water and should not be used directly. If you are unsure about using a crystal, use the indirect method for creating your essence (see opposite).

2 Prepare the crystals by washing and cleansing them with sage, palo santo or another method of your choosing.

3 Programme the stones by setting an intention or purpose for them. If you are using amethyst for its calming properties, for example, you may like to set an intention to help with anxiety or insomnia. If you are using citrine for its uplifting qualities, you may like to set an intention for attracting happiness, light and abundance.

4 Add your crystals to the glass of water and leave in sunlight or moonlight for at least one hour. You can leave them from sunrise to sunset or overnight on a full moon, if you like.

5 Remove the crystals and transfer the water to the jar, along with the vodka.

6 Fill your dropper bottle with ¾ fresh water and ¼ essence for easy use. For best results, crystal essences may be ingested or applied to the skin. You can take three to four drops twice a day.

THE INDIRECT METHOD

Some crystals are not suitable to use in essences directly. For stones that may be toxic, such as malachite or pyrite, use an indirect method for creating a crystal essence. This involves placing the stone in a separate glass or jar within the water so that it does not directly touch, but still absorbs its vibrational energy.

ROOM SPRAYS AND FACE MISTS

It is possible to make simple crystal-infused room sprays and facial mists to incorporate certain healing energies into your home or beauty routine. For both, begin by making a simple crystal-infused water by following steps one to four of the essence recipe opposite. Transfer your crystal-water to a spray bottle (but do not add any alcohol). For the room spray, add a few drops of your choice of essential oil to the bottle – the exact amount will depend on the choice of oil and your preference. For the face mist, add a few drops of moisturising oil (such as argan, almond or rose hip) along with your preferred essential oil.

TIP
You can also create crystal essences using oil instead of water, which is especially useful when making balms or salves for the skin.

Crystal Grids

Created by placing a selection of stones in a symmetrical pattern, a crystal grid is used for directing the flow of energy towards a specific purpose. It can be used to transform the energy within a space or for manifesting an intention. You can then charge the grid by setting an intention for it. Choosing crystals for your grid is an important part of the process. Use crystals that correspond with a goal or intention – you can choose them by colour or by their healing properties, as long as you are using your intuition and creativity.

Crystal Grid for Success and Abundance

This grid is designed to help you attract success and abundance into your life. Think of this example as a guide and remember to follow your own intuition when making a crystal grid.

WHAT YOU NEED

Clean flat surface

Sage smudge stick or palo santo wood

Lighter or matches

Crystals: 1 pyrite, 4 citrine, 4 rutilated quartz, 8 clear quartz

TIME

Depending on the size of your crystal grid, allow at least fifteen minutes for this ritual. You can leave your grid in place for as long as you like. Just remember to cleanse it occasionally and refocus on your intention.

METHOD

1 Cleanse the crystals you will be using, along with the space, using sage or palo santo.

2 Set your intention for the grid, giving the crystals a specific purpose, for example, 'I welcome success and abundance into my life'.

3 Start creating your grid starting with the main master crystal in the centre – in this case, pyrite.

4 Now take the four citrine crystals placing one either side of the pyrite, one above and one below. If they are points, face them outwards away from the centre.

5 Place the rutilated quartz crystals in between the citrine stones.

6 Now place each clear quartz crystal around the outside of the other stones to form a symmetrical pattern.

7 Lastly, complete the grid by focusing your energy on your intention. Centre yourself and visualize the outcome to begin the manifestation process.

> ### TIP
> You might also like to add other elements to this sacred space, such as candles, fresh flowers or incense.

Crystal Grid for Protection

Use this crystal grid as a way of absorbing negative energy from your space. A protection grid contains a powerful combination of crystals to help guard against any unwanted energy in your home.

WHAT YOU NEED

Clean flat surface
Sage smudge stick or palo santo
* wood*
Lighter or matches
Crystals: 1 obsidian, 4
* black tourmaline, 4 selenite, 8*
* clear quartz*

TIME

Depending on the size of your crystal grid, allow at least fifteen minutes for this ritual. You can leave your grid in place for as long as you like. Just remember to cleanse it occasionally and refocus on your intention.

METHOD

1   Cleanse the crystals you will be using, along with the space, using sage or palo santo.

2   Set your intention for the grid, giving the crystals a specific purpose, for example, 'I only attract positive energy into my home'.

3   Start creating your grid starting with main master crystal in the centre – in this case, obsidian.

4   Now take the four black tourmaline crystals placing one either side of the obsidian, one above and one below. If they are points, face them outwards away from the centre.

5   Place the selenite crystals in between the black tourmaline stones.

6   Now place each clear quartz crystal around the outside of the other stones to form a symmetrical pattern.

7   Lastly, complete the grid by focusing your energy on your intention. Centre yourself and visualize the outcome to begin the manifestation process.

Crystal Grid for Love and Relationships

This grid is designed to help you attract unconditional love into your life. The crystals used in this grid carry an uplifting and supportive energy that can be used to promote self love, as well as to attract new love into your life, or to support a current relationship with your partner.

WHAT YOU NEED

Clean flat surface
Sage smudge stick or palo santo wood
Lighter or matches
Crystals: 1 medium rose quartz, 4 rhodochrosite, 4 chrysocolla, 8 smaller rose quartz

TIME

Depending on the size of your crystal grid, allow at least fifteen minutes for this ritual. You can leave your grid in place for as long as you like. Just remember to cleanse it occasionally and refocus on your intention.

METHOD

1   Cleanse the crystals you will be using, along with the space, using sage or palo santo.
2   Set your intention for the grid, giving the crystals a specific purpose, for example, 'I welcome love and happiness into my life'.
3   Start creating your grid starting with main master crystal in the centre – in this case, rose quartz.
4   Now take the four rhodochrosite crystals placing one either side of the rose quartz, one above and one below. The distance between each stone should be equal so that the grid is symmetrical.
5   Place the chrysocolla crystals in between the rhodochrosite stones.
6   Now place each smaller rose quartz crystal around the outside of the other stones to form a symmetrical pattern.
7   Lastly, complete the grid by focusing your energy on your intention. Centre yourself and visualize the outcome to begin the manifestation process.

CHAPTER 4

FIND YOUR FIX

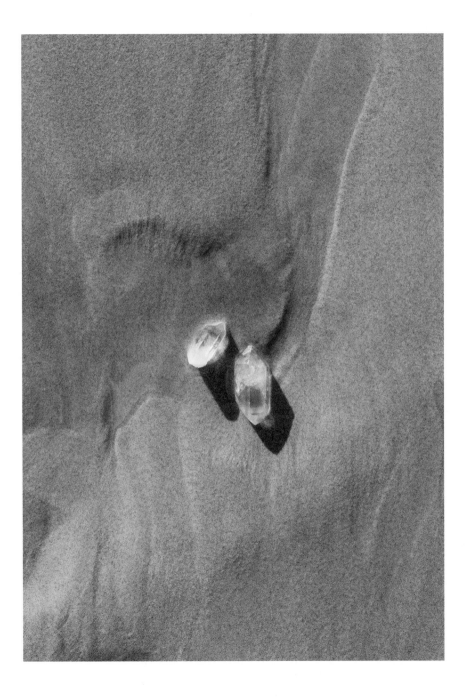

INDEX OF STONES BY NEED

GENERAL INDEX

Page numbers in **bold** refer to main directory entries

ACKNOWLEDGEMENTS

I would like to acknowledge and thank the following people for their endless encouragement and support during the writing of this book. You have all played an important role throughout the process, and I am so grateful to each and every one of you.

To my best friend and fiancé, Bali, for continuously supporting and encouraging me in all that I do. Thank you for your unwavering support, patience, love and genuine enthusiasm.

To my wonderful mother, Mallika, for so many things! Thank you for your endless encouragement, kindness, advice and support, not only through this process, but always.

To my beautiful sister, Dhyana, for being my number one employee. Thank you for always being ready to help at a moment's notice. Luminosity Crystals wouldn't be running without you!

To my first ever crystal suppliers, Kevin and Gwen, for always having such a strong knowledge and love of stones. Thank you for helping me to create my business in the very beginning.

My commissioning editor, Philippa Wilkinson, for your endless encouragement, advice and support throughout this entire process. I can't thank you enough for giving me the opportunity to turn my ideas into reality.

The White Lion Publishing team, thank you all so much for your hard work and dedication to this project. I couldn't be more grateful.

ABOUT THE AUTHOR

Juliette Thornbury first created Luminosity Crystals in 2015 from the hills behind Byron Bay, Australia. An idea based around her hope to share a little bit of the magic and wonder that Mother Earth provides, Luminosity Crystals has now grown into a thriving online shop and wholesaler, renowned for its sustainable and high-quality sourcing.